Valerio Alfonso Bruno, James F. Downes, Alessio Scopelliti

The Rise of the Radical Right in Italy
A New Balance of Power in the Right-Wing Camp

Valerio Alfonso Bruno, James F. Downes,
Alessio Scopelliti

THE RISE OF THE RADICAL RIGHT IN ITALY

A New Balance of Power in the Right-Wing Camp

Bibliografische Information der Deutschen Nationalbibliothek
Die Deutsche Nationalbibliothek verzeichnet diese Publikation in der Deutschen Nationalbibliografie; detaillierte bibliografische Daten sind im Internet über http://dnb.d-nb.de abrufbar.

Bibliographic information published by the Deutsche Nationalbibliothek
Die Deutsche Nationalbibliothek lists this publication in the Deutsche Nationalbibliografie; detailed bibliographic data are available on the Internet at http://dnb.d-nb.de.

Cover picture: Photo 38239033 © Massimo Valicchia | Dreamstime.com

ISBN (Print): 978-3-8382-1562-4
ISBN (E-Book [PDF]): 978-3-8382-7562-8
© *ibidem*-Verlag, Hannover • Stuttgart 2024
Alle Rechte vorbehalten

Das Werk einschließlich aller seiner Teile ist urheberrechtlich geschützt. Jede Verwertung außerhalb der engen Grenzen des Urheberrechtsgesetzes ist ohne Zustimmung des Verlages unzulässig und strafbar. Dies gilt insbesondere für Vervielfältigungen, Übersetzungen, Mikroverfilmungen und elektronische Speicherformen sowie die Einspeicherung und Verarbeitung in elektronischen Systemen.

All rights reserved. No part of this publication may be reproduced, stored in or introduced into a retrieval system, or transmitted, in any form, or by any means (electronic, mechanical, photocopying, recording or otherwise) without the prior written permission of the publisher. Any person who commits any unauthorized act in relation to this publication may be liable to criminal prosecution and civil claims for damages.

Printed in the EU

Table of Contents

Acknowledgements 7
Introductory note by the authors 9
Preface 11

PART ONE
Overview 17
1   The Italian Political Landscape 19
2   The 'Post-Berlusconi' Right-Wing Coalitions in Italy 33

PART TWO
Leading Actors of the Radical-Right Mainstreaming 67
3   (Northern) League's Case Study: A Text-Based Analysis of Matteo Salvini's Social Media Rhetoric 69
4   The Foundation, Rise and Affirmation of Fratelli d'Italia (2012-2022) 105
5   Electoral Volatility: The Post-2018 Electoral Decline of the Valence Populist M5S Party in Italy 139

PART THREE
The Future of the Italian Radical Right 161
6   The Italian Center-right Coalition and the Transnational Cleavage 163
7   One Year on from the 2022 Italian General Election 187

List of Abbreviations 203

Acknowledgments

The authors would like to especially thank their respective families for their tireless support during the writing of this book, which took more than three years to complete. The authors would also like to pay a special thanks to the publishers, ibidem Press and Columbia University Press for all their excellent support and editorial work throughout the writing of this book. The authors would like to especially thank Dr. Marianna Griffini, assistant professor in international relations and anthropology from Northeastern University London, for very kindly writing an excellent preface for this book, drawing on her extensive knowledge of Italian party politics alongside populism. Finally, the authors would like to pay a special tribute to colleagues and friends at the former Center for Analysis of the Radical Right (now known as the Far Right Analysis Network) and Polidemos, the Center for the Study of Democracy and Political Changes at the Catholic University of Milan, for all their tremendous and invaluable support over the years.

Introductory Note by the Authors

This book stems from research carried out over the past three years by the three authors on the role of the radical right in Italian politics. This study includes a wide range of perspectives to explore the rise of the populist radical-right within the Italian context of the last decade, roughly a ten-year period that ranges from the so-called *crisi dello spread* ('spread crisis') of 2011–2012 to the victory of the right-wing coalition led by Giorgia Meloni's party, Fratelli d'Italia, at the September 2022 general election. We argue that over the last decade, Italy has represented, and continues to represent, a laboratory for a number of political phenomena, such as technocratic governments, different forms of populism, especially those of the radical right or valence populism, alongside the complementary phenomenon of "mainstreaming" the far-right and the radicalization of traditional parties in Italian politics.

Could Italy, whose government is arguably the most right-wing government in the Republican history of the country lead to a new model at the European level? A model that would be based on a complex and gradual transformation between conservative and far-right ideologies, alongside a new political axis between the European People's Party and right-wing radical parties, such as The European Conservatives and Reformists Group (ECR) or Identity and Democracy (ID). On the eve of the election of the European Parliament to be held in early June 2024, we believe that these important and complex questions concerning Italian politics are significant for the future of both European and European Union (EU) politics alike.

The book consists of seven chapters[1] divided into three parts. The first part of the book serves as the backdrop for the entire book, offering a comprehensive examination of the complex Italian political landscape, exploring Italian political dynamics since post-

---

[1] Chapter 1 is carried out by James F. Downes and Alessio Scopelliti. Chapters 2 and 4 are carried out by Valerio Alfonso Bruno. Chapters 3 and 6 are carried out by Alessio Scopelliti. Chapter 5 is carried out by James F. Downes. Chapter 7 is carried out by Valerio Alfonso Bruno and Alessio Scopelliti.

World War II (Chapter 1) and focusing on the Italian Center-right Coalition (Chapter 2). The second part of the book focuses on actors that played a leading role in contributing to the normalization (or mainstreaming) of the Italian radical right, including the League (Chapter 3), Brothers of Italy (Chapter 4) and the Five Star Movement Party (Chapter 5). Finally, the third part of the book explores new areas that will impact Italian politics in the future via the new transnational cleavage (Chapter 6) alongside the mainstreaming of the Italian radical right (Chapter 7).

Milan and Hong Kong, October 2023

Preface

Marianna Griffini

Italy as a political lab is the image that takes shape when reading this highly topical book, which traces the emergence and incipient success of the radical right in Italy within the broader context of party competition both within and without this party family. The book, thanks to solid theoretical bases sophisticatedly corroborated by qualitative analysis of narratives and quantitative exploration of text, takes the reader through an in-depth investigation of the radical right historical background, actors, and dynamics, which have been animating the Italian political arena over the past three decades.

In *The Rise of the Radical Right in Italy: A New Balance of Power in the Right-Wing Camp*, the recurrent metaphor of a lab cogently conjures up Italy as a political field relentlessly experimenting with political phenomena, such as the short-lived technocratic governments led by European Central Bank Presidents Mario Monti (2011-2012) and Mario Draghi (2021-2022), and the normalization of the radical right. Technocratic governments breaking the chain between elected and electors have been deployed vastly in Europe, such as in Greece in 2011 and in Austria in 2019. Nevertheless, Italy was a forerunner. The same applies to the normalization of the radical right, which is made up of the radicalization of mainstream parties, the increasing acceptance of radical right tropes in the mainstream, and the entry into the government by radical right parties. The radical right presence in government is not unique to Italy, but Italy was one of the precursors of this trend that spread across Western, Central and Eastern Europe. Other radical right parties in power since Italy's first Berlusconi government (1994) have been the Austria Freedom Party (FPÖ) in 2000 and 2021; the Swiss People's Party (SVP) from 1959 to the present, with a brief hiatus in 2000; Fidesz in Hungary from 1998 to 2002, and since 2010; Law and Justice (PiS) in Poland from 2005 to 2007, and from 2015 to 2023; the Independent Greeks (ANEL) and SYRIZA in Greece in 2015.

Italy retains two additional roles in the Europe context. Indeed, it was home to the first populist government composed of a populist radical right and a valence populist party: the first Conte government (2018-2019). The Conte I government saw the populist radical right (originated as a regionalist party in 1989) Lega sitting uncomfortably in government with the 'polyvalent and eclectic' populist Movimento Cinque Stelle (M5S), aptly defined in Chapter 5 as the 'valence populist party'. The populist radical left SYRIZA in Greece had tied governmental knots with the nationalist and conservative ANEL in 2015, thus bringing together parties located far away from each other on the political spectrum; however, neither of those government coalition partners was a valence party transcending the ideological affiliation squarely to the right or left.

Moreover, Italy was home to the first totally populist radical right party in Western Europe, with the current Meloni government headed by Giorgia Meloni, the first woman prime minister in Italian history, leader of Fratelli d'Italia (FdI), and leader of the EU parliamentary group ECR. As illustrated in Chapter 2, the populist radical right Lega and Alleanza Nazionale (AN) had already featured in numerous governments in Italy under the aegis of Forza Italia's (FI) leader and tycoon Silvio Berlusconi (in 1994, 2001 and 2008). The Lega had also participated in the unusual coalition government Conte I, headed by M5S Giuseppe Conte (2018-2019). Therefore, unbeknownst to its actors, the Italian political scene set the stage for European political experiences of technocratic governments, of the now widespread normalization of the radical right often aided by social media platforms (as argued in Chapter 3), of the first government coalition in Europe between valence populism and radical right populism, as well of the first totally populist radical right government headed by a clearly populist radical right party.

Along with political experimentations, another trait characterizing the image of the Italian political lab shaped by this book is the fine balance between change and continuity. First, as Chapter 1 details, electoral volatility and political instability have triggered the changes that have punctuated Italian politics since 2000, which arose from the rubble of the political earthquake set off by the first of many political crises in Italian politics since 1992: *Tangentopoli*. The corruption scandal of *Tangentopoli* brought to an end the First

Republic party system dominated by the hegemony of the Socialist Party and the Christian Democrats, hanging in a fine but stable balance of power with an array of other parties, including the Italian Communist Party. Since the end of the First Republic, several political crises have seen governments being brought down before the end of their terms by contending parties. Indeed, political crises have curiously been a sign of continuity in the mercurial Italian political system.

A further essential and more unambiguous element of continuity in Italian politics since the 1990s is the constant presence of the radical right. The latter affirmed itself as a novel political actor at the beginning of the Second Republic by seizing the window of opportunity offered by potent discontent with the First Republic party system plagued by rampant corruption. The radical right, at that time constituted by the embryonic form of the Lega, AN, and FI, hailed itself as a game changer. The current radical right government led by FdI (the heir to the well-entrenched AN) is inevitably proving the unwavering presence of the radical right and portending the further changes the Meloni government may bring about. While Meloni has so far softened the most radical traits of her party, her radical positions on immigration, gender rights, law and order, and economic *souverainisme* may open up the possibility of a radical drift. The current fickle balance of power between the dominating FdI and its (reluctantly) junior coalition parties, Lega and FI, may also point in the direction of a reshuffled balance of power, relegating Lega and FI to the margins of the coalition and dwindling electoral fortunes. Only time will tell.

Italy as a lab is the fil rouge of the chapters unfolding in *The Rise of the Radical Right in Italy: A New Balance of Power in the Right-Wing Camp*. The core argument of this book is that the radical right in Italy has been undergoing an upward trajectory since 1992, which has seen the rise of new parties, such as FdI, the competition between radical right populism and valence populism (such as in the Conte I government), and within the radical right itself (i.e., the friend-and-foe competition between FdI, the FI, and the originally ethno-regionalist Lega). This variegated picture made up of chameleonic (but not meteoric) parties forms the balance of power of the radical right in Italian politics, which is methodically dissected by Bruno, Downes, and Scopelliti.

The purpose this book superbly achieves is to vividly trace the physiognomy of the radical right over *la longue durée*, as well as to deeply excavate the workings of its most crucial processes, including its normalization that has been built up across the past three decades and has peaked with the current Meloni government. Scholarly interest in these dynamics can depart from the case study of Italy (which served as the prototype of different radical right trends) before generalizing to relevant European radical right parties. Therefore, *The Rise of the Radical Right in Italy: A New Balance of Power in the Right-Wing Camp* offers a much-needed addition to the essential literature on party politics because it is of interest to the wider scholarly community studying radical right parties across Europe.

Recent developments in 2023 make the importance and significance of this book even more important. The radical right has hit the headlines for its (rare) lack of success, for instance, the recent dethronement of the PiS government after the October 2023 elections in Poland, but especially for its (relentless) success, exemplified by the rescuing of the Dutch Party for Freedom (PVV) Geert Wilders from the *cordon sanitaire* imposed since 2012. Wilders won the November 2023 elections and is set to enter negotiations for the formation of a coalition government. On the other side of the Ocean, Donald Trump, representing an unambiguously radical strain of Republicanism, announced his candidacy for the 2024 elections after having been acquitted from his second impeachment initiated on the grounds of incitement of insurrection in the attack on Capitol Hill on 6 January 2021. Trump's possible election carries the risk of democratic backsliding, which has already been initiated by Trump's Argentinian counterpart Javier Milei, who won the November 2023 elections at the helm of La Libertad Avanza. Curiously, the wildness of Wilders's, Trump's, and Milei's hirsute hairdos is matched by the brashness of their political style.

Returning to the European political milieu, the EU parliamentary elections have elicited a flurry of attention concerning EU right-wing parliamentary group alliances. There is trepidation about a possible instability in the balance of power within the

Italian radical right as a repercussion of its fragmentation at the EU level. Indeed, the radical right party ECR, which flaunts vigorous commitment to Euroskepticism, is getting closer to the European Popular Party (EPP), to which FI firmly belongs. The ECR, curiously, is spearheaded by Meloni, who took the party reins in 2020. With the advent of her institutional role as prime minister of Italy and her consequent attempt to maintain solid diplomatic relationships with the EU, Meloni reportedly toyed with the idea of edging closer to the EPP, which is, ironically, the EU parliament party she dragged FdI out of in 2019.

The precarious balance of power of the Meloni government could be thrown out of kilter also by Salvini's staged efforts at consolidating the EU parliament party ID, encompassing, among others, Le Pen's Rassemblement National in France, the PiS, the Austrian FPÖ, and the Dutch PVV. The EU elections will be a testing ground for the cohesion of the Meloni government, not just because of different EU parliamentary party affiliations of the government components but also because the EU parliament elections catalyze attention on the different party positioning within the radical right (recounted in Chapter 4) on the war in Ukraine. In fact, Salvini, heading the Lega and allegedly representing business people, expressed skepticism regarding sanctions on Russia. Instead, Meloni and Tajani (FI leader in the post-Berlusconi era) have been steadfast supporters of Ukraine and staunch opposers of Putin's Russia. Not only are the EU parliamentary elections concentrating pundits' attention on the radical right in Italy for their repercussions on the Italian government's balance of power, but they also highlight the pivotal role the radical right is playing well beyond Italian confines: the inter-party dynamics at play at a national level are taking an interesting turn at EU level. This makes the scholarly investigation carried out by Bruno, Downes, and Scopelliti even more urgent.

PART ONE
Overview

Chapter 1
The Italian Political Landscape

Post-WWII Italian Politics (history and constitution)

The First Republic (1948–1994)

As the main aim of this book is to understand the rise of the radical right in contemporary Italian politics, this chapter focuses on a historical perspective of Italian politics since 1945 that has shaped contemporary Italian politics in the 21st century. After the downfall of the Fascist political regime under Benito Mussolini and the end of World War II, Italian politics was radically transformed. In 1948, the First Republic (1948–1994) was officially established. During this period, Italy underwent a period of significant political, economic, and social change. The First Republic was characterized by the dominance of two political parties: the Christian Democratic Party (DC) and the Italian Communist Party (PCI). These political parties represented the two main ideological axes in Italian politics, with the DC representing the center-right and the PCI representing the center-left (see McCarthy, 2000; McCarthy, 1997).

Since post-WWII, Italy has been a parliamentary republic with a multi-party system, with the constitution in place since 1948. Article 1 of the Italian Constitution states that Italy is a democratic republic. Furthermore, Italy has a bicameral chamber that shares the same powers, with the Chamber of Deputies (Lower House) and the Senate (Upper House) with a president (head of state) and the prime minister, who is appointed by the president of the republic and must have the support/confidence of political parties in parliament to stay in office (see Newell, 2018; Newell, 2010; McCarthy, 1997).

The First Republic was also marked by a high degree of political instability, with frequent changes of government and coalition-building among the various political factions (see McCarthy, 2000; McCarthy, 1997). This was due in part to the proportional representation electoral system, which made it difficult for any one party to gain a clear majority in parliament. Despite the political instability, the First Republic was a period of significant economic growth and modernization in Italy. However, the First Republic was also marked by widespread corruption and clientelism, particularly in the south of the country. This created a sense of disillusionment among many ordinary Italian citizens and arguably contributed to the political instability that characterized the period (Katz, 1996).

Overall, the Italian First Republic was a complex period in Italian history, marked by political, economic, and social change, as well as challenges and opportunities for the country's democratic institutions (see McCarthy, 2000; McCarthy, 1997). The Italian First Republic ended due to a combination of factors, including political corruption, economic stagnation, and the end of the Cold War. Throughout the 1980s and early 1990s, Italy faced a series of corruption scandals that implicated many high-level politicians and members of the business elite. These scandals, collectively known as *Tangentopoli* (Bribesville), led to widespread public disillusionment with the political establishment and a loss of faith in the ability of the political class to govern effectively. At the same time, Italy was experiencing an economic downturn, with high inflation, low growth, and an ever-increasing public debt. This created a sense of economic discontent and a feeling of frustration among the population.

The end of the Cold War also played a role in the collapse of the First Republic. With the collapse of the Soviet Union, the ideological divide that had defined Italian politics for decades began to lose its relevance. This created an opportunity for new political forces to emerge, which challenged the traditional parties that had dominated Italian politics since the end of World War II. In 1992, a major corruption scandal involving the Socialist Party and its leader, Bettino Craxi, led to the collapse of the governing coalition and the formation of a new government.

In 1994, the First Republic officially came to an end with the election of Silvio Berlusconi and the formation of his center-right Forza Italia (Forwards Italy, FI) Party. Berlusconi represented a new type of politician, one who was not part of the established political class and who promised to bring a fresh approach to Italian politics.

Berlusconi's election in 1994 marked the beginning of a new era in Italian politics as the country moved away from the old system of clientelism and corruption that had characterized the First Republic (see Orsina, 2014; Newell, 2018).

The Second Republic (1994–)

The Italian Second Republic refers to the period of Italian history that began in the early 1990s, following the collapse of the First Republic and continues to the present day in 2023. The Second Republic has been characterized by significant political, economic, and social changes that have transformed Italy's political landscape.

The Second Republic was born out of the corruption scandals and political upheaval that marked the end of the First Republic. In the early 1990s, a series of corruption investigations, collectively known as *Tangentopoli*, led to the collapse of the traditional political parties that had dominated Italian politics since the end of World War II. This created an opportunity for new political forces to emerge and marked the beginning of a new era in Italian politics (see McCarthy, 2000; McCarthy, 1997).

One of the defining features of the Second Republic has been the emergence of political parties and movements, such as Silvio Berlusconi's FI, the populist, anti-establishment Five Star Movement, and the center-left Democratic Party. These parties have challenged the dominance of the traditional parties that characterized the First Republic and have brought new ideas and issues to Italian politics in the 21st-century political context (see Orsina, 2014).

The Second Republic has also been characterized by significant economic change, including neo-liberal economics, via the liberalization of markets and the privatization of state-owned enterprises. Crucially, the Second Republic has also faced significant challenges, including ongoing political instability and corruption, alongside economic stagnation and high levels of public debt. These economic challenges have tested Italy's democratic institutions and contributed to a sense of frustration and disillusionment among the Italian electorate. Most significantly, the Italian Second Republic has been a period of ongoing change and transformation in Italian history, marked by crucial challenges for the country's political and economic future (see McCarthy, 2000; McCarthy, 1997; Newell, 2010).

Volatility and fragmentation: The 21st-century political landscape in Italy

Since 2000, Italian politics has been marked by significant political instability and frequent changes of government. The period has been characterized by the emergence of new political forces, the decline of traditional parties, and ongoing challenges related to corruption, economic stagnation, and immigration (see Albertazzi and Vampa, 2021; Albertazzi and Zulianello, 2021).

In 2001, Silvio Berlusconi was elected prime minister for the second time, leading a center-right coalition that included his party, FI. Berlusconi's government implemented several economic and social reforms but was also marked by controversy and scandal, particularly related to allegations of corruption and conflicts of interest. In 2006, Romano Prodi, a center-left politician, was elected prime minister, leading a coalition that included the Democratic Party. Prodi's government tended to focus on economic reform and social issues but faced significant opposition from the center-right and struggled to maintain a stable majority in parliament (see Fella and Ruzza, 2013).

In 2008, Berlusconi was once again elected prime minister, leading a center-right coalition that included his party, FI. Berlusconi's second government was also marked by controversy and scandal. Furthermore, Berlusconi's government was largely criticized for its handling of the economic crisis that began in 2008. In 2011, Berlusconi resigned as prime minister due to increasing economic and political pressures. Berlusconi was replaced by Mario Monti, a technocrat who was appointed to lead a government of national unity during the severity of the economic crisis in Italy (see Orsina, 2014; Fella and Ruzza, 2013).

Monti's government implemented a series of economic reforms and austerity measures but faced significant opposition from the center-right and struggled to maintain its majority in parliament. In 2013, elections were held that resulted in a hung parliament, with no party or coalition winning a clear majority. After weeks of political disputes and machinations, a coalition government was formed between the center-left Democratic Party and the center-right People of Freedom Party, led by Silvio Berlusconi's protégé, Enrico Letta (see Fella and Ruzza, 2013). In 2014, Letta resigned as prime minister and was replaced by Matteo Renzi, a center-left politician who promised to bring a new approach to Italian politics. Renzi's government implemented several important economic and social reforms but continued to face significant opposition from both the center-right and the populist Italian Five Star Movement Party.

Between 2018 and 2023, Italy experienced three short-lived coalition governments (Garzia, 2019). The Giuseppe Conte I Cabinet (2018–2019) was formed between the Italian populist Italian Five Star Movement Party and the radical right League Party. The next coalition government featured the Conte II Cabinet (2019–2021) between the Five Star Movement and the center-left Democratic Party. After the failure of the Conte II Cabinet, the Mario Draghi Cabinet (2021–2022) featured a coalition of all different right-wing and left-wing ideologies with an eclectic technocratic-populist mix of political parties (see Chiaramonte, 2023; Chiaramonte et al., 2023).

The Draghi government collapsed in 2022, and a snap general election was called in Italy on September 25th, 2022. The Draghi government arguably collapsed due to a combination of factors, such as the withdrawal of key coalition partner support and disagreements over key policy issues on economic debt restructuring in the context of the COVID-19 pandemic and immigration. Furthermore, Draghi's refusal to lead a significantly weakened government and political opportunism by right-wing opposition parties such as FdI paved the way for another set of national elections (see Chiaramonte, 2023; Chiaramonte et al., 2023). Therefore, the collapse of the Draghi coalition government led to the snap general election in September 2022 that brought Giorgia Meloni's radical right FdI party alongside a right-wing coalition to power. We will more comprehensively address the rise of Meloni's FdI party in the September general election in the final chapter of this book (see Donà, 2022).

Key political parties in Italy

Italy has a multi-party-political system, meaning that many political parties compete for seats in the country's parliament. Political alliances and coalitions are common features of Italian politics, as no single party has traditionally been able to win a majority of the seats in parliament on its own. In recent years, key socio-cultural issues of political contestation, such as immigration and Euroskepticism (see Maggini and Chiaramonte, 2019; Pirro and Van Kessel, 2018), have become highly salient issues in contemporary Italian politics, alongside the unique role of populism (Zulianello, 2020).

Table 1 below provides a brief overview of the key political parties in Italy, alongside providing an overview of the recent electoral performances of the main political parties in Italy in the recent (a) national parliamentary election (2022 Italian general election) alongside (b) at the 2019 European Parliament election.[2]

Table 1.1   List of Main Political Parties in Italy

Party	Year Founded	Ideology	Party Leader	Deputies	Senators	Number of MEPs
Brothers of Italy (Fratelli d'Italia)	2012	Radical Right	Giorgia Meloni	118/400	66/200	9/76
Democratic Party (Partito Democratico)	2007	Center-left	Elly Schlein	69/400	38/200	15/76
Lega (League)	2017	Radical Right	Matteo Salvini	66/400	29/200	25/76
Five Star Movement (M5S)	2009	Valence Populist	Giuseppe Conte	52/400	28/200	6/76
Forza Italia (Forward Italy)	2013	Center Right	Vacant*	45/400	18/200	10/76

---

[2]   These are just a few of the major political parties in Italy, and there are many other smaller parties that also compete for seats in the Italian parliament.

Action (Azione)	2019	Center	Carlo Calenda	11/400	4/200	1/76
Green Europe (Europa Verde)	2021	Center-left	Angelo Bonelli & Eleonora Evi	6/400	1/200	1/76
Italian Left (Sinistra Italiana)	2017	Center-left	Nicola Fratoianni	4/400	3/200	0/76
Italia Viva (Third Pole)	2019	Center	Matteo Renzi	10/400	6/200	1/76

Notes: *As of 5 July, 2023

Below is a brief overview of some of the major political parties in contemporary Italian politics:

The Democratic Party (Partito Democratico, PD): The Democratic Party is a center-left political party that was formed in 2007. The Democratic Party has been in power several times since its original founding in 2007. The Democratic Party's ideology primarily focuses on issues such as social democracy, progressivism, and positive support for the EU (see Bordandini et al., 2008). The Democratic Party has been deeply critical of radical right parties in Italy, such as The League and Brothers of Italy parties. On socioeconomic issues, the party has tended to focus on the big state via supporting policies for a strong welfare state and higher levels of taxation.

The Five Star Movement (Movimento 5 Stelle, M5S): The Five Star Movement is a populist, anti-establishment party that was founded in 2009. It has a strong anti-corruption platform and has tended to gain support from voters who are dissatisfied with the traditional left-wing and right-wing political parties in Italy (see Zulianello, 2020).[3]

---

[3] The Italian Five Star Movement Party will be explored more comprehensively in Chapter 5 of the book, via an analysis of the party's recent electoral decline amidst the wider context of the rise of the radical right in 21st century Italian politics.

Forza Italia (Forward Italy, FI): Forza Italia is a center-right party that was founded in 1994 by former Prime Minister Silvio Berlusconi. The party has been in power several times since its formation (see Orsina, 2014). FI's core party ideology has tended to focus on a strong emphasis on law and order, alongside adopting conservative positions on issues such as abortion and same-sex marriage. In terms of socioeconomic positions, the party has tended to adopt a free-market-based position.

Lega Nord (Northern League): Lega Nord is a radical right political party that was founded in 1991. The party has traditionally advocated for greater autonomy for the northern regions of Italy and has taken a strong anti-immigration position in its core party strategy. In recent years, the Northern League has rebranded its party ideology, dropping the name 'Nord' (North) and rebranding itself as Lega (The League) in December 2017. The current party leader is Matteo Salvini, who has served as party leader since 2013 (see Albertazzi et al., 2018).

Fratelli d'Italia (Brothers of Italy, FdI): In comparison to the League Party, Fratelli d'Italia is a new radical right party that was founded in 2012. The party is known for its nationalist and anti-immigration views, alongside having gained support from voters who are dissatisfied with mainstream political parties on both the left-wing and right-wing of the political spectrum (see Donà, 2022). The current party leader is Giorgia Meloni, who also currently serves as the Italian prime minister (since October 2022).

Italia Viva: Italia Viva is a center-left party that was founded in 2019 by former Prime Minister Matteo Renzi (who was the prime minister for the Democratic Party between 2014 and 2016). Italia Viva adopts liberal policies and has been critical of both the Democratic Party and the Five Star Movement in recent years. In addition, Italia Viva has tended to adopt both pro-EU positions alongside pro-immigration positions.

Key concepts of the book

The normalization of the far-right through electoral consent

The European political landscape has witnessed a constant transformation in recent years, with far-right parties establishing themselves as pivotal players in both national and transnational politics. This shift is not a temporary phenomenon but rather a consistent trend in which far-right parties have evolved from momentary electoral phenomena (often interpreted as protest votes) into viable electoral alternatives in many European countries. This transformation is evident both at the national level (see, e.g., the Austrian Freedom Party, Vlaams Belang, Freedom and Direct Democracy, National Rally, Alternative for Germany, the League, Brothers of Italy, the Dutch Party of Freedom, Vox and Sweden Democrats) and within the European Parliament (see, e.g., Identity & Democracy and European Conservatives & Reformists). These electoral results reflect a broader shift in European politics toward a more prominent presence of far-right ideologies within the demand side of party politics. For that reason, this book aims to provide further explanations on how far-right ideas, values and norms are becoming more normalized from a supply-side perspective. Accordingly, the Italian political landscape presents an ideal laboratory to explore the rise and normalization of far-right parties. Indeed, in the 2018 general elections, the League emerged as the leading force in the center-right coalition, alongside Brothers of Italy and Forward Italy. This electoral success culminated in the formation of the most right-wing, populist, and Euroskeptic government in the history of the Italian Republic: the I Conte Cabinet.

Most significantly, this Italian electoral result indicates that far-right ideas are no more to be considered outrageous or stigmatized, but they are rather normalized and accepted by much of the Italian electorate. Italian far-right parties are viewed as representatives of their electorates' ideals and interests rather than as means to express a vote for protest against mainstream parties. Therefore, by exploring the political dynamics at play in Italy, this book will provide valuable insights into the evolving political landscape of far-right parties within contemporary European politics.

Conceptualization of radical right parties

Before delving into the structure of this book, it is necessary to clarify what we mean by the term radical right parties. We already referred to the well-known phenomenon of far-right mainstreaming. However, while referring to parties such as League and Brothers of Italy, this book employs the term 'radical right' (and not extreme right-wing parties) to investigate the unique characteristics and dynamics associated with these parties. This categorization places them within the right-wing political spectrum, specifically beyond the center-right, but not reaching the extreme fringes (Gattinara and Pirro, 2019; Mudde, 2019). Contemporary radical right party ideology encompasses three distinctive core ideologies: nativism, authoritarianism, and hostility toward liberal democracy.

Nativism, the first defining feature of radical right parties, centers on the belief that a nation-state should exclusively comprise members of the native group (Rydgren, 2018) and the exclusion of non-native elements (Triandafyllidou, 1998; Rovny, 2013). Authoritarianism, the second critical core ideology, advocates for strict state control to ensure security and order within the country's borders (Adorno, 1950; Flanagan and Lee, 2003; Mudde, 2007: 22-23). Consequently, loyalty to the (native) group and the leaders in power is expected from all individuals within the nation. The third component is the hostility toward liberal democracy. Betz and Johnson (2006) note that this hostility need not always be explicit, but radical right parties do not hesitate to employ it. For instance, once in government, radical right parties do not hesitate to implement policies that facilitate forms of majoritarianism, reinforcing the executive body of democratic regimes over the other two bodies (legislative and judiciary) (Mudde, 2013, 2014; Wintrobe, 2018; Castillo-Ortiz, 2019; Urbinati, 2019).

The main distinction between radical right parties and extreme right-wing parties primarily lies in their approach to liberal democracy (Carter, 2018). On the one hand, radical right parties, while seeking power, generally abstain from violence. On the other hand, extreme right-wing parties embrace violence as one of their core ideologies and ways of doing politics. However, it is essential to acknowledge that this non-violent approach of radical right parties does not diminish their potential threat. Due to their inherent opposition to the values of liberal democracies, radical right parties continue to pose a danger to contemporary democracy and societal stability (Scopelliti et al., 2021).

References

Adorno, T. W. (1950). *The authoritarian personality*. New York: Harper & Brothers.

Albertazzi, D., and Vampa, D. (Eds.). (2021). *Populism and new patterns of political competition in Western Europe*. London: Routledge.

Albertazzi, D., and Zulianello, M. (2021). Populist electoral competition in Italy: the impact of sub-national contextual factors. *Contemporary Italian Politics*, 13(1), 4-30.

Albertazzi, D., Giovannini, A., and Seddone, A. (2018). 'No regionalism please, we are Leghisti!'The transformation of the Italian Lega Nord under the leadership of Matteo Salvini. *Regional & Federal Studies*, 28(5), 645-671.

Betz, H. G., and Johnson, C. (2004). Against the current stemming the tide: the nostalgic ideology of the contemporary radical populist right. *Journal of Political Ideologies*, 9(3):311-327

Bordandini, P., Virgilio, A. D., and Raniolo, F. (2008). The birth of a party: the case of the Italian Partito Democratico. *South European Society & Politics*, 13(3): 303-324.

Carter, E. (2018). Right-wing extremism/radicalism: Reconstructing the concept. *Journal of Political Ideologies*, 23(2), 157-182.

Castelli Gattinara, P., and Pirro, A. L. (2019). The far-right as social movement. *European Societies*, 21(4), 447-462.

Castillo-Ortiz, P. (2019). The illiberal abuse of constitutional courts in Europe. *European Constitutional Law Review*, 15(1), 48-72.

Chiaramonte, A. (2023). Italy at the polls. Four lessons to learn from the 2022 general election. *Contemporary Italian Politics*, 15(1), 75-87.

Chiaramonte, A., Emanuele, V., Maggini, N., and Paparo, A. (2023). Radical-Right Surge in a Deinstitutionalised Party System: The 2022 Italian General Election. *South European Society and Politics*, 1-29.

Donà, A. (2022). The rise of the Radical Right in Italy: the case of Fratelli d'Italia. *Journal of Modern Italian Studies*, 27(5), 775-794.

Fella, S., and Ruzza, C. (2013). Populism and the fall of the center-right in Italy: The end of the Berlusconi model or a new beginning? *Journal of Contemporary European Studies*, 21(1), 38-52.

Flanagan, S. C., and Lee, A. R. (2003). The new politics, culture wars, and the authoritarian-libertarian value change in advanced industrial democracies. *Comparative Political Studies*, 36(3), 235-270.

Garzia, D. (2019). The Italian election of 2018 and the first populist government of Western Europe. *West European Politics*, 42(3), 670-680.

Katz, R. S. (1996). Electoral reform and the transformation of party politics in Italy. *Party Politics*, 2(1), 31-53.

Maggini, N., and Chiaramonte, A. (2019). Euroskepticism behind the Victory of Euroskeptic Parties in the 2018 Italian General Election: Not Exactly. *JCMS: Journal of Common Market Studies* 57: 77-89.

McCarthy, P. (1997). *The crisis of the Italian state: from the origins of the Cold War to the fall of Berlusconi and beyond*. London: Palgrave Macmillan.

McCarthy, P. (Ed.). (2000). *Italy since 1945*. Oxford: Oxford University Press.

Mols, F., and Jetten, J. (2020). Understanding support for populist radical right parties: toward a model that captures both demand-and supply-side factors. *Frontiers in Communication*, 5, 83.

Mudde, C. (2013). *Are populists friends or foes of constitutionalism?* Policy brief. The Foundation for Law, Justice and Society. Oxford: Oxford University.

Mudde, C. (2014). Fighting the system? Populist radical right parties and party system change. *Party Politics*, 20(2), 217-226.

Mudde, C. (2019). *The far-right today*. Hoboken: John Wiley & Sons.

Newell, J. (2010). *The politics of Italy: Governance in a normal country*. Cambridge: Cambridge University Press.

Newell, J. L. (2018). *Parties and democracy in Italy*. London: Routledge.

Orsina, G. (2014). *Berlusconism and Italy: A historical interpretation*. New York: Springer.

Pirro, A. L., and Van Kessel, S. (2018). Populist Euroskeptic trajectories in Italy and the Netherlands during the European crises. *Politics*, 38(3), 327-343.

Rovny, J. (2013). Where do radical right parties stand? Position blurring in multidimensional competition. *European Political Science Review*, 5(1), 1-26.

Scopelliti, A., Downes, J.F. and Bruno A.V. (2021), Can You Tell an Authoritarian From a Fascist? *Fair Observer.*

Triandafyllidou, A. (1998). National identity and the 'other'. *Ethnic and racial studies*, 21(4), 593-612.

Urbinati, N. (2019). *Me the people.* Cambridge: Harvard University Press.

Wintrobe R. (2018), An economic theory of a hybrid (competitive authoritarian or illiberal) regime. *Public Choice*, 177(3–4), 217–233.

Zulianello, Mattia (2020). Varieties of populist parties and party systems in Europe: From state-of-the-art to the application of a novel classification scheme to 66 parties in 33 countries. *Government and Opposition*, 55(2), 327-347.

Chapter 2
The 'Post-Berlusconi' Right-Wing Coalitions in Italy

The Italian right-wing coalition at the 2022 general election

The latest Italian general election, held on September 25, 2022, saw the victory of the right-wing coalition, with 43.79% and 44.02% of the preferences obtained in the Chamber of the Deputies and the Senate of the Republic (Chiaramonte and De Sio, 2024). The election was characterized by a high level of abstention (lowest turnout ever, at under 64%)[4]. The party FdI led by Giorgia Meloni obtained in both the Houses overall an excellent performance, with around 26% of preferences, while Matteo Salvini's League resulted weakened, with about 8,8%, followed closely by Silvio Berlusconi's FI, slightly above 8%[5]. On the other hand, the center-left coalition, led by the PD, obtained about 26% of the electoral preferences in the two Houses of Parliament. In comparison, the Movimento Cinque Stelle (M5S) reached 15.5% and Azione-Italia Viva, a recent political party labeled as *Terzo Polo* (Third Pole), about 7.7%, led by Carlo Calenda and former PM Matteo Renzi, respectively.

Notwithstanding the excellent performance of FdI, overall, the victory for the right-wing coalition was less overwhelming than expected, as in the past, similar Berlusconi-led coalitions have reached from 45 to 49%. In this sense, the much-feared 'massive turn to the Right' by the Italian electorate did not happen, de facto showing a certain continuity with the past (among others, Albertazzi et al., 2021). However, it is undeniable that there has been an intra-coalition balance shift between the political subjects of the coalition, i.e.,

---

[4] Ansa (Italy) Election: turnout lowest ever at under 64% Nine points lower than in 2018, https://www.ansa.it/english/news/politics/2022/09/26/election-turnout-lowest-ever-at-under-64_ffa88f14-dd7f-4299-9861-7d2ba742ac18.html, accessed 29 September 2022.

[5] More precisely, 8,27% at the Chamber of the Deputies and 8,11% at the Senate of the Republic.

from League to FdI, continuing a process that had already begun several years ago, in particular since 2018, which can be traced back further to the crisis which led to the resignation of the fourth Berlusconi cabinet in November 2021. So, as there has not been the much-heralded massive turn of the Italian electorate to the (extreme or far) Right, it is at least possible to say that the current political coalition leading Italy is certainly much more rightward-centered than it used to be (among others, Castelli Gattinara and Froio, 2021). Very eloquently, though, the current right-wing coalition in Italy continues to be widely referred to as the center-right coalition (*coalizione di centrodestra*) within the Italian public debate (Bruno, 2022).

In this chapter, we look at the Italian right-wing coalitions that emerged in the period that we may define as post-Berlusconi. It is important to highlight that, as mentioned above, the party led by Berlusconi started losing its central influence within the right-wing bloc since the late 2011 *crisi dello spread* (spread crisis).

Between the summer and fall of 2011, in the frame of the European sovereign debt crisis and the long wave of the global financial crisis, which started in 2007–2008, austerity measures imposed by the Troika on Greece also threatened Italy and the fourth Berlusconi government[6]. Mario Draghi and Jean-Claude Trichet (at the time, the newly appointed president and former president of the ECB, respectively) sent a letter to the Italian authorities urging them to reform Italy's welfare system, tax system, and labor market, with Italy's government debt at about 120% of its GDP at the time (2011). Furthermore, the European Commission (EC) demanded a letter of intent, with the spread Btp-Bund exceeding 400 and Berlusconi having no longer credit vis-à-vis foreign chancelleries. The then president of the republic, Giorgio Napolitano, opted to intervene with an unusual communiqué, urging the government's action in the frame of guidelines that had come from the EU. On November 8, with the spread breaking through the 570 ceiling, Berlusconi

---

[6] In the European Union context, the Troika represented, according to the European parliament website, the set of official creditors during negotiations with countries, and consists of representatives of the EC, the ECB and the International Monetary Fund (IMF).

went up to the Quirinale to explain why the vote on the *rendiconto dello Stato* in the House had passed with only 308 votes. The next day, Napolitano named Mario Monti a senator for life, and on November 12, Berlusconi resigned, leading the way to a technocratic executive led by Monti.

We know that about one year after this crisis, the party FdI was founded by Giorgia Meloni, Ignazio La Russa and Guido Crosetto, while Matteo Salvini was appointed leader of the Lega Nord in late 2013. In late 2013, the project of the Popolo delle Libertà (The People of Freedom), established in 2008–2009 to bring together FI and Gianfranco Fini's AN, miserably failed.

The Italian right-wing bloc between 1994 and 2022 and the role of Forza Italia

We can now move on to compare the overall share of votes obtained by the current right-wing coalition at the Italian general election held in September 2022 with past performances of the right-wing blocs. It is worth mentioning that since 1994, with the exception of 1996, right-wing parties and center-right parties have been able to unite during general elections. When we talk of the political parties comprsing Italy's right-wing bloc from 1994, we are talking mainly in relation to the following three political parties:

a) Forza Italia (1994–2008 and 2013–)
b) Movimento Sociale Italiano (MSI), later AN[7], and FdI[8]
c) Lega Nord (since 2017 Lega per Salvini premier)

---

[7] The Popolo delle Libertà (PdL) was launched by Silvio Berlusconi as an electoral list, including Forza Italia and Alleanza Nazionale, on 27 February for the 2008 Italian general election and was dissolved in November 2013. In 2008 general election the PdL obtained 37.4% of the votes (with 46.8% for the right-wing coalition), while in 2013 it obtained 21,6% of the votes, without the recently established FdI, with the coalition obtaining 29.2%. On the context that surrounded the creation of FdI see the chapter of this book: "Foundation, Rise and Affirmation of Fratelli d'Italia (2012-2022)".

[8] See Chapter four on this. See also Vassallo and Vignati (2023), Vampa (2023) and Broder (2023).

It is important to compare the overall performances at the general elections of the right-wing bloc since 1994 and to look at the specific electoral performances of the parties composing it.

Table 1. Electoral results of the center-right coalition (main parties) between 1994 and 2022, general elections (% vote) at the Camera dei Deputati (The Chamber of Deputies).

Year	Forza Italia	MSI-AN-FdI	Lega Nord/Lega per Salvini Premier	Center-right coalition (combined)
1994	21	MSI 13.5	8.4	42.9
1996	20.6	AN 15.7	10.7 *Not part of the coalition*	42.1
2001	294	AN 12	3.9	49.6
2006	23.7	AN 12.3	4.6	49.7
2008	PDL 37.4		8.3	46.8
2013	PDL 21,6	FdI 1.9	4.1	29.2
2018	14	FdI 4.4	Lega 17.4	37
2022	8.1	FdI 25.98	Lega 8.79	43.79
2023*	6.5	FdI 29	Lega 10	45.5[9]

As can be seen from Table 1, the right-wing coalition that won in the latest general election did not reach the results achieved by other comparable coalitions led by FI under the leadership of Silvio Berlusconi, which had been close to 50% (as in 2001 and 2006) or more than to 45% (as in 2008). It is, therefore, already possible to say that it is not true that Italy has voted massively in favor of the right in recent years or that there has been a turn to the far-right of Italian citizens. However, what remains a matter of debate is whether it can be said that the current right-wing coalition is more radical than the previous ones. Indeed, the nature of the 'core' or leading party of the previous coalitions, i.e., FI (and then the People of Freedom for a while), led by Silvio Berlusconi (who passed away

---

[9] The 2023 is based on late October 2023 opinion polls. In particular: https://www.adnkronos.com/politica/sondaggio-politico-fratelli-ditalia-ancora-primo-partito-stacca-di-9-punti-il-pd_5ZD1tFM8xS94DRZ2edJmFk and https://sondaggibidimedia.com/sondaggio-swg-23-ottobre/

in June 2023), is controversial. It is certainly true that in recent times, FI, which resumed its activities in 2013 after the brief Partito della Libertà (PDL) parenthesis, had indeed insisted on increasingly labeling itself as a moderate, liberal, and pro-European party (Bruno, 2022).

For instance, in the last election campaign held during the summer of 2023, FI, for the first time, included the words 'Partito Popolare Europeo' (EPP) in its logo is notable, as it is something that has never been done before (figure 1)[10]. Regarding this, FI MP's Mauro D'Attis said: "Forza Italia is a genuinely pro-European party and the reference to the EPP in the symbol with which it will run in the next election underlines our firm anchorage to the values of the largest political family in the EU. This is our home, that of the moderates, of which in Italy, thanks to the leadership of President Berlusconi, we are an authoritative and inimitable expression. Be wary of imitations" [Authors' translation].

---

[10] On Forza Italia newest logo, see: https://www.rainews.it/articoli/2022/08/forza-italia-presenta-il-simbolo-con-berlusconi-presidente-e-riferimento-al-ppe-0327f693-ffad-4f8f-b041-a0a0784aa887.html

Figure 1. On the left is the logo of Forza Italia for the 2018 general election. On the right is the new logo of Forza Italia (2022) with the words Partito Popolare Europeo on the top.

To analyze the specific nature or the ideology of the party FI (see among others: Albertazzi and Newell 2015; McDonnell 2013; Paolucci 2006; Pasquino 2003; Raniolo 2006) does not into the scope of this chapter; however, it is undeniable that, despite recent attempts such as the one just mentioned to give itself a façade of 'moderation', notable elements of right-wing radicalism and populism have gone mainstream under Silvio Berlusconi political life. It suffices to mention that the MSI was included and, in fact, 'cleared' politically for the first time in 1994, precisely by virtue of Berlusconi's decision to run together with Gianfranco Fini's MSI/AN, or the fact that during the 2022 election campaign Berlusconi on live TV, reported that the war in Ukraine was the responsibility of the Ukrainians and not Putin, whom he described as a friend and a good person[11] (Bruno and Fazio, 2023).

---

[11] As Bruno and Fazio (2023) have showed, among others, Forza Italia's positioning vis-à-vis the issue of support for Ukraine has always been controversial. As for the Draghi government crisis, while it is true that it was triggered by the Five-Star Movement in relation to a number of dossiers, including military support for Ukraine and the annual defense budget, it is undeniable that Forza Italia and the League themselves contributed to the downfall of the government headed by the former president of the European Central Bank, saying that they would no longer support a government also formed by the Five-Star

Beyond the debate about the radical elements introduced by FI, which make us lean toward a certain continuity at the level of right-wing coalitions from 1994 to the present, it is also true that the 'post-Berlusconi' coalitions that participated in the last two general elections of 2018 and 2022 saw a dramatic shift within the coalition in terms of power dynamics. Between 1994 and 2013, as Albertazzi et al. (2021, 181) pointed out, "Voters were also clear as to where the center of the right-wing galaxy was to be found: to adopt an astronomical metaphor, it was occupied by 'the Berlusconi sun'"; starting in 2018, however, the 'sun' position of the right-wing galaxy was occupied, for a relatively short period, by Salvini's League

Movement. Lately, on at least two other occasions Berlusconi has been very vocal about his position in relation to Russia and Ukraine. The first was during the TV program 'Porta a Porta' on 22 September 2022: "Putin fell into a difficult and dramatic situation, he fell because it was a mission of the two pro-Russian republics of the Donbas that went to Moscow and talked to everyone, to newspapers, TV and party ministers, they went to him in delegation saying ... Zelensky increased the attacks of his forces against us and our borders, we came to 16.000 dead, defend us because if you don't do it we don't know where we can get to, thus Putin was pushed by the Russian people, his party and his ministers to come up with this special operation". The second time, on 18 October 2022, in an audio recording (we do not know if recorded without Berlusconi's knowledge or not), it is possible to hear the president of Forza Italia stating, among other things, that: "The Russians feel at war with Italy because Italy gives weapons to Ukraine". Then he says he is worried and has rekindled relations with Putin thanks to twenty bottles of vodka and a "very sweet" letter, adding "I was declared by him the first of his five true friends". To remedy this delicate situation concerning the relationship with the United States, Berlusconi then issued a statement on 19 October blaming the Italian Left: "In 28 years of political life, the Atlantic choice, Europeanism, the constant reference to the West as a system of values and alliances between free and democratic countries have been the basis of my commitment as a political leader and a man of government. As I explained to the United States Congress, friendship and gratitude to that country are part of the values to which my father was educated as a boy. No one, I stress nobody, can afford to question this. The Left, which has so often been on the wrong side of history, certainly cannot afford to do so. Nor was the Left of the Democratic Party, which even in the last elections, less than a month ago, was allied with the enemies of NATO and the West. All this, however, would not exist, if there were not in Italy the bad habit of transforming political discussion into gossip, using stolen phrases recorded secretly, and notes photographed with mobile phones, with a method not only unfair but intimidating". In conclusion, as for the League, statements and declarations by Silvio Berlusconi on Russia and Ukraine (but not only), may they be voluntarily or not, risk to jeopardize Italy's right-wing coalition and the Meloni executive in the next months.

(Albertazzi et al. 2018), and then by FdI itself starting in 2022. What is next?

The 'post-Berlusconi' right-wing bloc: reshuffle of power or radicalization?

Is it possible to note that the 'post-Berlusconi' right-wing blocs led first by Matteo Salvini and then by Giorgia Meloni are more radical than their predecessors under Silvio Berlusconi? To analyze the alleged dynamics of radicalization within the latest right-wing coalitions in Italy, we now focus closer on the League and FdI while we leave aside FI, whose future role under the leadership of Tajani is uncertain, with the possibility that the party without Berlusconi will be either incorporated/federated with FdI (or, much less probable, by the Lega) or dissolve.

Examining the complex dynamics behind the radicalization of the mainstream and the mainstreaming of the far-right, Bruno and Downes (2023) have recently argued that both FdI and Lega, and in particular their leaders Matteo Salvini and Giorgia Meloni, have been the drivers of this shift of Italian politics toward the far-right of the political spectrum. In addition, they have also sought to keep a political façade of respectability and relative moderation. In this direction, the League prefers label of *sovranista*, and FdI uses 'conservative'[12] to identify both Giorgia Meloni's and the party's ideological positioning. For these reasons, far-right rhetoric, alongside the use of extreme right-wing narratives and slogans, and the continuous nods to the most conservative corners of Catholicism have all been deployed and yet are tolerated without much fanfare in the Italian public debate.

Moreover, it is important to highlight once again the importance of the 'realm' of policies and policy-making alongside institutional communications. In contrast, public narratives, during political campaigns, make up a completely different 'realm' (on this debate, see among others Vassallo and Vignati 2023). However,

---

[12] Yet, in the official logo of FdI for the 2024 EP election, both the wordings *sovranisti* and *conservatori* appears.

symbols and slogans have their value; in particular, they play a role in the radicalization of mainstream politics and the 'mainstreaming' of the extreme right. This is true also for Salvini's League and Giorgia Meloni FdI. For instance, in a 2022 report, Bruno (2022b) found evidence that when it comes to the use of online slang, slurs, codes and key phrases, the populist radical-right in Italy, i.e., the League and FdI (and media outlet closely associated to them, such as 'La Voce del Patriota') and extreme-right movements and groups such as Casa Pound and Forza Nuova, to mention few, are hard to distinguish. The line between the two can often be blurred. In a famous campaign poster, Matteo Salvini was depicted (Bruno 2022b, 36) with the following slogan that reads: "STOP! BUREAUCRATS, BANKERS, DO-GOODERS AND BOATS".

Figure 2. A poster from the League political campaign for the election of the European Parliament (26 May 2019). It reads: "STOP! BUREAUCRATS, BANKERS, DO-GOODERS AND BOATS". Source: https://www.facebook.com/legasalvinipremier/photos/stop-burocrati-banchieri-buonisti-e-barconi-meno-5-domenica-26-maggio-dalle-7-al/2372409512801961/.

As concerns 'Burocrati', both the mainstream populist right and far-right movements in Italy have the EU as a target, especially the 'Brussels bureaucrats'. The main difference lies in the fact that while the latter maintains an attitude of naked and hard Euroskepticism, the former alternates between strong criticism of the European institutions, especially the EC, and moments of softer Euroskepticism. In the case of Salvini's League, starting with the Draghi government (February 2021), it is possible to say that the component of Euroskepticism has almost disappeared but will most probably come back during the next political campaign. The use of the slang 'banchieri' (bankers) in a negative and allusive sense (bankers' servants or bankers' waiters) is well documented as far as the current Italian radical and extreme right is concerned. It is used widely by both the mainstream radical right, the League and Brothers of Italy and extreme-right neofascist movements and groups (for instance, Movimento Fascismo e Libertà). As far as the mainstream right is concerned, however, a fundamental difference can be seen starting with the election of Mario Draghi, former president of the ECB, as prime minister in February 2021. Notably, Salvini's League, part of Draghi's government, has begun to use the slang 'bankers' less and less for obvious reasons of political opportunism. 'Buonisti' (do-gooders) is a slur used by both the mainstream populist right and the far-right in Italy. The do-gooders would be the representatives of the left that, in a purported hypocritical way, favor, at least according to the radical right, illegal and uncontrolled immigration, the criminality that threatens the order of the citizens and of the Italian armed forces.

Moreover, the 'buonisti', in the narrative of the Italian radical right, are often intellectuals and elites remote from the people, who secretly favor a homologation that would lead to the loss of concepts such as identity, homeland, nation and traditional family. 'Barconi' (Barges) is the sadly well-known word used by the Italian media to describe the makeshift boats often used by immigrants, upon payment of large sums of money to criminal organizations, to arrive clandestinely on Italian coasts, particularly from North Africa. However, some Italian radical-right politicians have made 'barconi' slang to identify an allegedly uncontrolled invasion of

Italy's borders by illegal immigrants. Matteo Salvini, in particular, became known for exploiting the issue strategically, with an intense campaign while he held the role of minister of the interior in the so-called 'yellow-green coalition' (first Conte government June 2018–September 2019).

Talking about symbols and slogans in relation to the radicalization of Italian politics and mainstreaming of the far-right, and following Bruno (2022b) and Bruno et al. (2021), we may ask about the role of the 'Fiamma Tricolore' in FdI symbology.

Figure 3. On the left is the Tricolor Torch ['Fiaccola Tricolore'], a symbol first used by Young Italy [Giovane Italia], the youth wing of the MSI or Italian Social Movement between 1954 and 1971. On the right, the Tricolor Flame [Fiamma Tricolore], the symbol of the MSI, established in 1946 by veterans of the Repubblica Sociale Italiana, including Giorgio Almirante (1914–1988), and lately incorporated in 1995 in the party Alleanza Nazionale. Source: https://it.wikipedia.org/wiki/Fiaccola_tricolore. (See Bruno 2022b, 14).

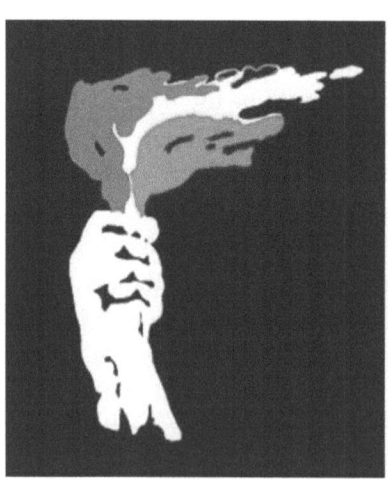

As Bruno argues (2022b, 13-14), with the tricolor flame, it is possible to move from symbols that can be considered properly 'fascist' to symbols that can be labeled as 'neofascist'. In particular, the MSI and its youth wing, 'Giovane Italia' (Young Italy), first adopted the tricolor torch, while the MSI has adopted the tricolor flame since at least 1948. The symbol of the tricolor flame has since moved to the AN party, established in 1995 under the leadership of Gianfranco Fini, until 2009, when Silvio Berlusconi's Popolo della Libertà absorbed the party. The flame has appeared in the logos of Brothers of Italy only since 2014, first in that of AN and, since 2017, by enclosing the tricolor flame *tout court*, as can be seen by the current logo of the party led by Giorgia Meloni (Figure 19), now displaying the tricolor flame visible in the center of the logo.

Figure 4. The current party logo of Brothers of Italy (2017–present). The one on the right includes the name of Giorgia Meloni. The MSI tricolor flame is clearly displayed in both. Source: https://www.fratelli-italia.it/tesseramento/.

The current Italian right-wing camp: two players on the same platform?

Once again, a key question to ask is whether the post-Berlusconi right-wing coalition governments, since 2018, are indeed more radical than previous ones. Albertazzi et al. (2021) and Albertazzi and Zulianello (2022) have argued that these trends concern more a reshuffle of power and roles within the Italian rightwing camp than a real process of radicalization of Italian politics, considering the recent results at the September 25, 2022 general election in Italy as a zero-sum game dynamic between populist radical-rights parties, i.e. FdI and Salvini's Lega. Castelli Gattinara and Froio (2021) have pointed out the process of gradual radicalization within the right-wing bloc that has been carried out in the last decade by the League and FdI: "... Following the failure of the PDL and the 2011 dramatic change of government, the political right has increasingly turned toward electorates sympathizing with authoritarian and nativist ideals associated with the silent counter-revolution (2021, p. 22), with the [...] predominance of radical parties over the Italian mainstream right posing some serious challenges over the fundamentals of liberal democracy in Italy" (Castelli Gattinara and Froio 2021, p. 23). Here, it is important to underline the distance between public narratives used more and more often, not only in electoral campaigns but in policies when in charge of the executive.

Concerning the relationship between radical and institutional/mainstream elements within Salvini's League, Bruno and Downes (2023) have argued that several core features can be identified in defining Salvini's party, granting important flexibility[13]. A first feature represented by the 'historical' League, the ideological core includes deeply entrenched roots in Northern Italy, which was for many years the key bastion of support for both Umberto Bossi and Roberto Maroni. This component, although currently latent, should not be underestimated (see the Lega Nord: Albertazzi and McDonnell 2005; 2009; 2010; Passarelli and Tuorto 2018; and Tarchi 2003)[14].

---

[13] On the League see Chapter three of this book: "(Northern) league's case study: a text-based analysis of Matteo Salvini's social media rhetoric".

[14] As Matto Salvini was elected federal secretary of the (then) Lega Nord in late 2013 he started to transform the party from a classic ethno-regionalist typology into a nationalist, sovereigntist, populist and radical-right one. Since 2018 in particular, Salvini ideologically rebranded and renamed the party as Lega—Salvini Premier or simply Lega, cutting off the word "North" and—consequently—abandoning the fundamental question of the independence of the so-call "Padania" (i.e. an aggregate of several northern regions for the independence of which the—once—Northern League fought for) (Bruno and Cozzolino, 2022).

A second feature that can be considered part of the contemporary League is expressed, for instance, by the party's support of the government by Mario Draghi between 2021 and 2022. This component is well represented by the current Italian Minister for Economic and Finance, Giancarlo Giorgetti, who may be considered one of the most pro-European and business-friendly policy-makers of the League[15]. This political shift is even more ironic, considering how the populist radical-right League has historically adopted a 'hard' Euroskeptic stance (i.e., outright rejection of the EU Project) and now bears much more ideological resemblance to that of a 'soft' Euroskeptic party (i.e., seeking to reform the EU Project from within/via the mechanisms of the European Parliament).

A third core feature of the League relates to that hard, extreme right-wing element of the party. In essence, this ideological element consists of creating structured links with the extreme right, not only neofascist but also neo-Nazi style links and allegations. This dynamic has been discussed, for instance, in a very interesting investigation by an online newspaper and in the investigations by Berizzi (2021), which have emphasized, for example, the fundamental role of the extreme right-wing group founded in 2010 in Lombardy, *Lealtà Azione*, in supporting the League with thousands of votes, with the promise of including its members in the party staff.

Finally, a fourth core feature resembles an ideological complexity, with the more properly pragmatic and populist core represented by the leader Salvini himself[16]. This ranges from the 'governing contract' (contratto di governo) with the M5S, with whom the League formed the 'yellow-green government' (see Coticchia 2021) led by Giuseppe Conte (Conte I cabinet) up to its sudden collapse. The new government (Conte II cabinet, 2019), based on a new alliance between the PD and M5S, gave birth to a different

---

[15] This is exemplified by the support of important European funds, around €220 billion, that Italy is currently using under the name of the PNRR (Piano Nazionale di Ripresa e Resilienza) (The National Recovery and Resilience Plan) or suggested the possibility of a "Semi-Presidenzialismo di fatto" (de facto Semi-Presidentialism) under Draghi.

[16] Salvini has on several occasions de jure or de facto disavowed the above-mentioned components, alongside finding a delicate balance that allows these ideologically disparate groups to coexist amongst one another.

parliamentary majority or support for the above-mentioned Draghi government. It is worth mentioning that at the time, all political parties supported Draghi's appointment except Giorgia Meloni's FdI, the only opposition party. Even the League, notoriously a Euroskeptic and anti-immigration party, agreed to support the new executive. In this respect, Salvini declared: "I rather prefer to play the game and manage 209 billion euros than not" — a clear reference to the Italian share of the Next Generation EU (NGEU) plan agreed in July the year before. In the days that saw Draghi being sworn in as Italy's new PM, the League was polling at 23%, its last time as the country's leading political party. In exactly two years, the League moved from a pre-pandemic 30.7% (January 2020) to 8.7% (September 2022), passing from being the leading political party in Italy to a position where it is behind not only FdI but also PD and M5S.

It is possible to say that starting around the time of the COVID-19 pandemic, a zero-sum game that sees votes lost by the League as votes won by FdI begins to take place (Vampa 2023; Vassallo and Vignati 2023). FdI and Lega have been, and are also currently competing, on a very similar political platform. This platform is composed of an electorate seemingly sympathetic to far-right ideologies or harboring a vague nostalgia for fascism, with politics of memory playing a key role (Griffini 2023; see also Newth and Maccaferri 2023). Meloni's party has a competitive advantage over Lega on the same populist radical-right and/or far-right platform. FdI is a relatively young party, founded in December 2012; however, it has a long ideological and historical tradition, unlike Lega, which has distanced itself from its former manifestation, the Lega Nord.

Also, as we already mentioned, FdI remained in opposition throughout the entire legislature (2018–2022), particularly against the yellow-green government during 2018–2019 and during Mario Draghi's executive (2021–2022), two executives that included Lega. It should not be underestimated that, albeit more moderately than its coalition ally, FdI has presented this narrative to Italian citizens as an example of its consistency and coherence with its principles and history. On a different but closely related point, the leadership of Giorgia Meloni, particularly her tenacity, consistency, and, to some extent, her *sui generis* idealism, may be good ingredients for building a narrative to help differentiate her from the much more chameleonic and pragmatic attitude of her colleague, Matteo Salvini.

So, if pragmatism and radical-right wing populism can be considered core features of Salvini's new League, what can be said about FdI? For FdI, the debate is more complex[17]. Vassallo and Vignati (2023) set out precisely this argument in several places in their monograph devoted to FdI. Although FdI's positions as of 2019 would prove a progressive radicalization, ascribing the party to the family of radical right-wing populist parties, would more properly describe FdI as fascist national-conservatism. The authors view FdI as the 'third party of the flame', following in the footsteps of MSI and AN. Not only is FdI deeply rooted within the democratic system, but it also appeals to a significantly larger voter base than its predecessors. In contrast to the original group of disenfranchised individuals and those who clung to memories, who had established MSI in the aftermath of World War II, FdI has managed to create a more inclusive and diverse community. Due to this stance, the authors advise refraining from any association with fascism by categorically steering clear of terminology like neofascist and post-fascist[18].

Adhering to this perspective, which originates from what the authors describe as 'context hermeneutic' as opposed to 'text

---

[17] On FdI see Chapter four of this book: "Foundation, Rise and Affirmation of Fratelli d'Italia (2012-2022)".

[18] A whole debate would indeed deserve the problem of the post-fascism category within Italian contemporary politics. We have seen the very convincing and detailed reconstruction of post-fascism given by Newth (2022) and Newth and Maccaferri (2022), starting from the political history of the Lega Nord to the current Lega, of post-fascism as a sui generis political logic used by far-right parties and leaders, thus not only FdI, in order to allow the mainstreaming/normalization of fascist and neofascist ideas and theories while at the same time defining themselves as "post-ideological" and fascist as an ideology belonging to the past and not existing anymore. Likewise, Broder (2023), has pointed at the historical process of gradual equivalence, implemented over decades by far-right actors in Italy, between anti-fascist resistance and fascism, with the relative trivialization of the first in favor of the second, that has allowed a party to define itself as conservative while clearing and normalizing characters, slogans and theories (once real taboos).

hermeneutics' (Vassallo and Vignati 2023, 257), it is evident that although certain aspects of connections with the past still linger, these connections predominantly possess symbolic or rhetorical attributes. This is often manifested in the form of verbal extremism and/or conspiracy-driven interpretations of global events and situations[19]. Vampa, in his *Brothers of Italy: A New Populist Wave in an Unstable Party System* (2023), has certainly the merit of clarifying concepts often used with great lightness and excessive ease. His interpretation brilliantly moves, showing the elements of rupture and continuity with the tradition of FdI, combining elements typical of the parties of the populist radical-right family (PRRPs, see on this, at least, Mudde 2004, 2007 and Zulianello 2020) with a long tradition, defined as post-fascist. Indeed, the characteristic elements of radical right-wing populist parties are the tendency to lack value and respect attributed to minority rights (illiberalism), nativism and authoritarianism. In contrast, the anti-democratic element and the use of violence for political ends would be the prerogative of the extreme right[20].

FdI's identification with the large 'conservative' family, by the way, has been advanced several times before. As early as 2020, Francesco Giubilei in *Giorgia Meloni. La rivoluzione dei conservatori* (2020) suggested a positioning reading for the party that, while holding firmly to its right-wing roots, embraced the conservative world. In fact, according to Giubilei, first, the entry into the ECR group and then the election of Meloni as president of the European Conservatives marked the beginning of a new political season for the construction of a great Italian and European conservative right. Discussing FdI's alleged radicalization, Donà has interestingly argued that the party's ideology turned to radical right positions after 2017, the year of the Trieste Congress. According to Donà, "... Since 2017, FdI platforms introduced R.R.P.'s elements of nationalism, nativism, and authoritarianism with the adoption of anti-EU

---

[19] Donà (2022) argues that the party, starting from a more moderate stance soon afterward its foundation in late 2012, soon embarked on a different path, respectively towards a national-conservatism and progressive radicalization.

[20] The debate on the use of far-right as umbrella concept has been suggested recently by Pirro (2022).

stances to exploit the electoral opportunities resulting from the ongoing Italian political instability and the misconducting of the European economic and immigration crises".

Those findings confirm the relationship between distinct crisis situations and the rise of R.R.P.s, given their capacity to use the crisis as a window of opportunity to gain electoral visibility and political influence. Puleo and Piccolino (2022) mostly remark on the discontinuity associated with FdI, with the party having accomplished a major ideological rebranding, positioning itself as radically different from both the mainstream center-right and the post-fascist tradition of the Italian Right. Indeed, it is undeniable, in retrospect, that the entry of FdI members into the European Group of Conservatives and Reformists, which was created for quite different purposes, facilitated a reading tending to increasingly accredit the party as being part of the conservative family, thereby separating it from more overtly identitarian and nativist radical right groups. Supporting this approach is the programmatic use widely and systematically of the term conservative by the leader herself. In the aforementioned autobiography, Meloni (2021) reiterates in a chapter titled "Conservare il futuro" (preserving the future) that she never intended, in order to ingratiate herself with a part of the establishment, to aim for a modern and dialogical right wing that would abandon its unpresentable positions, a mistake that would have been made instead by Gianfranco Fini (2021, 192–193)[21]. In this sense, the radicalization of the mainstream parties and the

---

21   Broadening the discourse, this interpretation moves within a trend of possible "alignment" or "convergence" between parties that we can describe and define as far-right and conservative parties, globally. It is not possible here, for obvious reasons, to show precisely the dynamics behind such convergence, however, these can be traced to (a) a strategic element implement by FdI but also to (b) a process, long and gradual, of gradual normalization and mainstreaming of issues, ideas, radical right features of public debate. The Italian case is thus exemplary in that it shows the dual dynamics of a process of normalization that starts from afar but has been placed increasingly strategically lately. Starting from the latter, it is therefore clear that the possibility of crediting FdI, both in Italy and abroad, as a party that is not only part of a conservative pan-European group (at least according to its name), but that even leads it, has a very important value. On the concept of mainstreaming see Mondon and Winter 2020. On conservatives and conservativism see Invernizzi and Sanguinetti (2023).

normalization of the far-right can be seen as a strictly interrelated and gradual process that can be found in several contexts, as it will be seen shortly.

Bruno (2022) has, among others, posed the question of the similarities and differences between FdI and Lega, but starting from a slightly different platform (i.e., far-right); FdI, unlike Lega per Salvini Premier, has a much older and deeper historical and ideological tradition (MSI, AN). The MSI was the Italian neofascist party par excellence, a movement founded in 1946 by veterans of the Italian Social Republic, including Giorgio Almirante (1914–1988) and Pino Rauti (1926–2012), at least up to the 'svolta di Fiuggi' of 1995, when the MSI allegedly found its way under the 'arco costituzionale' (constitutional arch), i.e., it became a political actor fully accepted and operating within the Italian rule of law and constitution (on this see Ignazi, 1994, 171–190). A brand-new name was subsequently chosen: Alleanza Nazionale or AN (National Alliance). However, the symbol of the tricolor flame migrated to AN's logo until Gianfranco Fini, in March 2008, accepted the federation into Berlusconi's Popolo della Libertà (People of Freedom, PDL). In 2014, the flame reappeared in the FdI logo after a six-year absence (Bruno 2022, 174–175). Subsequently, Bruno argues (2022, 180): "[…] Which of these two parties, FdI or Lega, which are competing on a very similar political platform (as we have seen from the political manifesto of FdI), will an electorate which is seemingly sympathetic to far-right ideologies or, as has recently been said, harbouring a vague nostalgia for fascism, choose to vote for? We believe most will favor FdI over Lega. After all, to put it very bluntly, why would a certain type of voter vote for a 'copy' when they can have the 'originali'?"

In relation to post-fascism, Bruno, Downes and Scopelliti (2021) discussed in a short article titled "Post-Fascism in Italy: "So why this flame, Mrs. Giorgia Meloni?" the role of a symbol as the *Fiamma Tricolore*":

> "[…] It is evident that [the] Brothers of Italy party has been adopting an increasingly ambiguous stance toward its fascist heritage. First of all, at the national level, the party does not seem to abandon any opportunity to employ aggressive strategies in attacking members of the academia through a

barrage of criticism and parliamentary questions because they dared to define Brothers of Italy a 'fascist' or 'neo-fascist' party. Secondly, at the local level, the party has never failed to flaunt its sympathy toward nostalgia of fascism during (online)public assemblies of representative bodies. [...] If the Brothers of Italy self-identify as a post-fascist party, what is the need to include this clear reference to the party's specific historical and political experience? The tricolor flame has always been a symbol, so evocative and powerful, that has passed through the years and the minds of the Italian electorate on par with the crusader shield of the Christian Democracy party and the hammer and sickle of the Communist party. This logo is, indeed, recognized by the Italian electorate as 'tacit connection' with the fascist regime while referring to the 'cult of the dead' and the funerary imagery [[...]] providing a potential space both for memory investments and emotional projections. However, when Brothers of Italy was founded in 2012, Giorgia Meloni did not use the tricolor flame in the party's logo. Perhaps, similar to other far-right parties in Western Europe, the reason to avoid this symbol was to overcome the stigma (2) of being associated with right-wing totalitarian regimes and attempting to be, rather, perceived as 'normal' or mainstream in the eyes of its electorate. Yet, Brothers of Italy employed (by stealth) this symbol in 2014 with a 'matryoshka' style (an old party logo with the flame, within the current party logo) and, then, it clearly showed the tricolor flame in the logo of the party since 2017. In short, considering the historical and political background of the tricolor flame, what we are asking in Italy and abroad is the following question: 'So why this flame, Mrs. Giorgia Meloni?'" (Bruno et al. 2021).

The Italian right-wing coalitions between radical-right populism and souverainism. Insights from public narratives vis-à-vis global financial markets

What are the ideologies that can be linked to the political actors that form the bulk of the recent Italian right-wing coalitions? (in particular, 2018 and 2022). As we discussed earlier on in the book, ideology includes the two right-wing parties that have picked up the 'baton' left by FI and Silvio Berlusconi from 2018 to the present day situation. Likewise, it is complex to ascertain whether these current right-wing coalitions are more radical than those of the past. It is conceivable that the process started with the end of the fourth Berlusconi cabinet, and the *crisi dello spread* (spread crisis) of late 2011 has *de facto* made Italy a European-level laboratory for the role of populism and technocratic governments. We do not dwell here on the role of a party such as the Five Star Movement, which will be addressed in detail in another chapter of the book, nor on the role of technocratic governments such as Monti's and Draghi's (see Chapter Four).

What we now want to attempt is a comparison at the level of public narratives (Coticchia and Catanzaro 2023; Coticchia and D'Amato 2018; Coticchia and Di Giulio 2023) by right-wing political leaders and members of the Italian executive in the last decade vis-à-vis financial markets. We can specifically consider the statements and interviews of Giorgia Meloni, Silvio Berlusconi, Giulio Tremonti, Roberto Maroni, Matteo Salvini, and Giancarlo Giorgetti vis-à-vis the role of financial markets. We can start from the most recent period and then move to the periods of the spread crisis (2011-2012) and yellow-green government by Lega and M5S (2018-2019).

Giorgia Meloni (9 February 2023 — Sole 24 Ore interview)

> .".. with Minister Giorgetti we are working to secure our debt from new financial shocks and attract the confidence of savers and investors, even in the medium term. We want to reduce dependence on foreign creditors by increasing the number of Italians and residents in Italy who hold shares of debt. Let me add an element: the only way to make a high debt like ours sustainable is through economic growth, not the blind austerity policies seen in past years". [22]

Giorgia Meloni (14 August 2023 — AGI)

> "The idea of the tax on banks' extra-profits is mine, mine is the political responsibility. It's a choice I would make again. I don't want to punish the banks, but there is an imbalance". [23]

Giancarlo Giorgetti (20 September 2023 — event by the Minister for Institutional Reform and Simplification)

> "What scares me are not the assessments of the EU but those of the markets that buy government debt. I wake up every morning and I have a problem:

---

[22] Translation from Italian by the author. Source: https://www.ilsole24ore.com/art/meloni-2023-rivoluzione-fiscale-piu-titoli-stato-detenuti-italiani-AEtOT3jC

[23] Translation from Italian by the author. Source: https://www.agi.it/politica/news/2023-08-14/meloni-tassa-extraprofitti-banche-22623255/

I have to sell government debt and I have to be catchy to get people to trust me". [24]

Matteo Salvini (14 September 2023 — Italian TV Rete 4)

"The ECB giving a damn about the economic difficulties of households and businesses raises the cost of money. Lagarde lives on Mars".[25]

Matteo Salvini (23 September 2023 — League congress in Genoa)

"There is a gentleman who some people call a philanthropist, who is one of the democratic problems of our country named Soros who spends billions to erase the culture of our country." [[...]] open society foundation, is Soros' way of channeling billions to associations whose goal is to erase the culture of Western civilization that we have won".[26]

Giorgia Meloni (September 29, 2023 — press conference at Malta Med9 meeting)

"The usual people would like a technical government and the Left already has a list of ministers. [[...]] The spread going up? I see this concern mostly in the wishes of those who imagine that a democratically elected government that is doing its job that has stability and a strong majority, should go home, replaced by a government that nobody chose. I really enjoy the debate, already the names of ministers and technical governments are being mentioned [[...]] The usual people would like the technical government and the Left already has the list of ministers. [[...]] I fear that this hope will not translate a reality. [[...]] Italy remains solid, it has a growth forecast above the European average even for next year, higher than France and Germany. [[...]] I want to reassure: the government is fine, the situation is complex. We handled it seriously last year and this year. The spread, which you are throwing around today as if it was the end of the Meloni government, was now at 192 points. Last October it was at 250, during the year before the new government it was higher, and I did not see any news the headlines. I know how to read politics and I know how to read reality: the Left keeps making

---

[24] Translation from Italian by the author. Source: https://www.huffingtonpost.it /economia/2023/09/19/news/giorgetti_mercati_spread_tassi_interesse_bce_ patto_ue-13387966/

[25] Translation from Italian by the author. Source: https://www.ansa.it/sito/noti zie/politica/2023/09/14/bce-salvini-lagarde-vive-su-marte_ff3949f0-4fca-4a3 4-981f-2cb3ec4294ce.html

[26] Translation from Italian by the author. Source: https://video.repubblica.it/ed izione/genova/salvini-dal-palco-della-lega-a-genova-attacca-soros-e-uno-dei- problemi-democratici-del-nostro-paese/453122/454085.

the list of ministers in the technical government, in the meantime we govern".[27]

Giorgia Meloni (Sallusti and Meloni 2023 – book interview)[28]

[[...]] Now, until before finance became a global factor, Italian government bonds were mainly bought by Italian citizens who, because of this, became a little richer and used this wealth in consumption or investment in Italy. [[...]] This has not been the case for many years, and today a good part of our debt is in the hands directly or indirectly of foreign banks and funds. [[...]] We cannot rule out the possibility that they buy our bonds abroad -- I am not referring to the individual private investor, but to the large entities scattered around the world – may from one day to the next decide not to buy them back, or even sell them suddenly, for reasons that may not even have to do with economic interest alone, but with other issues, and objectively put us in difficulty. [[...]] Here I simply point out how it is clear that too much debt in foreign hands can become a powerful weapon to interfere in the policies of sovereign states, especially those like us with such high debt. [[...]] 'Crisi dello spread' and public narratives vis-à-vis financial markets (2011-2012).

Roberto Maroni (November 22, 2011, Libero/Radio interview)[29]

[Giorgio Napolitano's move to send Mario Monti to Palazzo Chigi was] "a great deception to take out Berlusconi and his government. [...] It was said that the resignation of Berlusconi's government was enough and the spread would go down. Instead, it did not, instead".

Silvio Berlusconi (December 12, 2012, Corriere della Sera interview)

"I said it was a hoax in November 2011 and I confirm it because on a spread over 500 points a battle was waged in Europe blaming me and it was said that we had brought the country to the brink and that was a lie. Somebody said that state pensions and salaries could not be paid, the salaries were paid and I don't think the technicians had brought them the money into the government treasuries".

---

[27] Translation from Italian by the author. Source: https://www.adnkronos.com/politica/giorgia-meloni-sinistra-ha-gia-lista-ministri-per-governo-tecnico_21p5CvpQBbWhTJtp4OZxer

[28] Translation from Italian by the author. Source: Sallusti and Meloni 2023, 209-210.

[29] Translation from Italian by the author. Source: https://www.ilgiornale.it/news/maroni-va-allattaccomonti-e-inganno-fare-fuori-cav.html

Giulio Tremonti (2019 interview on Italy's 2011 crisis)[30]

"In the days of Curzio Malaparte ('Tecnica del colpo di Stato' 1931) coups were done with the crack of firearms, with guns in the palaces, later also with tanks in the squares, in more modern times they are done with the crack of spreads. Even in Greece they voted [...]in Italy they did not! What is tragic is that since then, and then to follow, Italy has lost increasing shares of its sovereignty. And perhaps we should (at least we could) begin to reflect on this, too, in search of the origins of our 'sovereignism' and a different idea of Europe".
'Governo giallo-verde' and public narratives vis-à-vis financial markets (2018-2019)[31]

Giancarlo Giorgetti (12 August 2018 — Libero interview)

"By the end of August the hedge funds will attack us, what happened to Berlusconi seven years ago may happen again. [[...]] And the opposition, in crisis, will do everything to jump on us. Europe and the elites fear this government. The attack [[...]] I expect it, the markets are populated by hungry hedge funds that pick their prey and act. We saw what happened in late August in '92 and seven years ago with Berlusconi. In summer there is little movement in the stock exchanges; it is a preparatory period for aggressive moves against states. But if the storm comes, we will open the umbrella. Italy... is a great country and has the resources to hold up, also thanks to its large private savings. What worries me is that, in the general silence, a large part of Italian savings has been taken abroad and therefore the management of our securities is not domestic".[32]

Giorgia Meloni (24 March 2019 — Twitter)

---

[30] Translation from Italian by the author. Source: https://www.ilsole24ore.com/art/colpi-stato-il-crepitare-spread-AC8zUR8
[31] At the Italian general election of March 2018, the Five-Star Movement (M5S) led by Luigi Di Maio obtained, rather unexpectedly, about 32% of the seats at the Chamber and the Senate. After three months of talks, the M5S formed with the League led by Matteo Salvini, a populist coalition government, led by the independent Giuseppe Conte (yet linked to the M5S) as PM. The yellow-green government of M5S and Lega can certainly be considered the one with the highest rate of populism in Italy's republican history, and at the time, with the country having a public debt of about 135 percent of its GDP, alliance partners and EU institutions were greatly alarmed. In the meantime, the spread Btp-Bund went back to the alarming rate of above 300.
[32] Translation from Italian by the author. Source: https://www.agi.it/politica/giorgetti_fondi_speculativi_giorgetti-4261669/news/2018-08-12/

"Soros funds Emma Bonino's +Europa (NDA, an Italian political party) with 200,000 euros. Keep the moneylenders' money, our strength is the Italian people".[33]

Giorgia Meloni (12 August 2020 — Facebook)

"For George Soros I would be an enemy of the EU. Instead, I think the real enemies of Europe are those who speculate on people's misfortunes, those who finance mass immigration and destabilize the society and culture of entire peoples. It just so happens that these are all characteristics that the 'philanthropist' so appreciated by the homegrown globalist left takes on. If fighting these drifts means being an enemy to Soros, then I am proud to be one".[34]

Matteo Salvini (22 May 2020 — Facebook)

"To be attacked by Mr. Soros, unscrupulous speculator and enemy of Italy, supporter of illegal immigration and funder of ultra-leftist NGOs, is for me an honor and a medal!".[35]

A comparative framework for right-wing (and valence) populist and souverainist public discourses vis-à-vis financial markets is provided here. We follow the ideational approach's definition of populism (Mudde 2004; Mudde and Rovira Kaltwasser 2017) *as a thin-centered ideology that considers society to be ultimately separated into two homogenous and antagonistic groups:* 'the pure people' and 'the corrupt elite' and argues that politics should be an expression of the volonté générale (general will) of the people. As concerns souverainism, a commonly accepted definition is less easy, yet following Mueller and Heidelberger (2020), Verzichelli (2021) and Scopelliti and Bruno (2023, 194), it is possible to frame it as "opposition to phenomena such as globalisation and Europeanism, including their respective elites, which would have allegedly taken

---

[33] Translation from Italian by the author. Source: https://www.repubblica.it/politica/2022/08/24/news/giorgia_meloni_definisce_soros_un_usuraio-362763770/.

[34] Translation from Italian by the author. Source: https://www.facebook.com/38919827644/posts/per-george-soros-sarei-un-nemico-della-ue-io-invece-penso-che-i-veri-nemici-dell/10158497441592645/.

[35] Translation from Italian by the author. Source: https://www.iltempo.it/politica/2020/05/22/news/matteo-salvini-stronca-george-soros-onore-essere-attaccato-da-speculatore-ultrasinistra-nemico-italia-finanziere-preoccupato-leader-lega-ue-europa-euro-1327488/

the original sovereignty away from the nation, an idealized place and time in which sovereignty (as political power, disposing of full control over a given territory, its borders, policy-making, etc.) belong to the nation".

As can be observed from the analysis of the statements, we have many narratives focusing on conspiracy theories (by 'evil technocrats', 'powers acting in the shade or poisoning the country', 'using immigration and NGOs') or 'insensitivity' by EU institutions, allegedly not caring about the country. There are also antisemitic tones. Financial elites and markets appear as blackmailing the country and shrinking its democratic exercise. Nonetheless, in the more recent statements and interviews, since FdI has become the fact the leading force of the right-wing coalition that won the 2022 general election, the narratives are slightly different. The focus now is more on reducing the dependence of the nation on foreign creditors, although at least since 2011, as Giorgetti states, "a large part of Italian savings has been taken abroad and therefore the management of our securities is not domestic". In synthesis, from the analysis of the statements above, it emerges (a) that Italian political leaders and politicians have often been using populist and souverainist narratives; (b) the current period, starting from August 2023, seems rather similar, in terms of narratives, to the ones of the late 2011 *crisi dello spread* and 2018, with the 'yellow-green' government by M5S and Lega; (c) somehow a discourse is gradually emerging, apart from the right-wing classic discourse (the interviews of Giorgetti and Meloni are telling). Even if it is objectively often impossible to distinguish between right-wing or valence populist[36] narratives and sovereignist ones, we believe that what makes the sovereignist discourse stand out should not be underestimated, i.e., the emphasis on diminishing dependence from foreign investors by increasing domestic residents who hold shares of debt, in order to avoid global financial markets depriving the nation of its sovereignty over public finance.

---

[36] Following Zulianello (2020) we can define valence populism as the one of parties pragmatic and ambivalent that changes positioning not ideologically but instrumentally (typical example is the first M5S in Italy).

Table 3. A comparative framework of Italy's populist and souverainist narratives (2011-2023)

Ideology	Key elements	Subject	Polemical target(s)	Examples of public narratives
Populism (right-wing and valence populism)	Society separated into two homogenous and antagonistic groups: 'the pure people' and 'the corrupt elite'; Politics should be an expression of the volonté générale (general will) of the people	The People	The elites, including: Financial elites (e.g. George Soros, Mario Monti, Mario Draghi)	Financial elite as: -corrupted and greedy, either enemy or do not care of the people; poisoning the country; - allied with the Left; promote globalization and immigration in order to erase the culture of Western civilization;
Souverainism	Nation as idealized place and time in which sovereignty (political power, disposing of full control over a given territory, its borders, policy-making, etc.) belongs to the people of the nation	The Nation	Phenomena taking the original sovereignty away from the nation (e.g., globalization, Europeanism), including financial markets and financial institutions (e.g., ECB)	Global financial markets: -deprive the Nation of its sovereignty over public finance; - may act in the shadow to overthrow democratically elected governments; The Nation should: -decrease dependence on foreign investors; -increase the number of Italians and residents in Italy who hold shares of debt;

Conclusion

In the conclusion of this chapter on center-right coalitions in Italy, a few points can be stated: the place that was occupied for years, starting in 1994, by Silvio Berlusconi and his FI party, has recently been occupied (briefly) by Salvini's new League. As early as late 2019, as we have shown, the zero-sum game for the electorate that sympathizes with the far-right and the politics of memory and nostalgia has seen FdI gradually prevail over the League. At the same time, with Silvio Berlusconi's demise in June 2023, the trend that FI was now a minor partner within the coalition's new balance of power was definitively enshrined. Obviously, if Salvini's League's position of 'hegemony' within the coalition was very short-lived and ephemeral, we can wonder how long that of FdI and Giorgia Meloni will last. One year after winning the September 2022 general election, the Meloni government (as will be seen in other chapters of this book) seems to have been able to hold its own through a strategy of low-budget 'culture wars' in the domestic sphere and an almost total alignment at the foreign policy level, in perfect continuity with the Draghi government and the past Italian executives.

It is possible to argue that there are differences between past and more recent Italian right-wing coalitions; however, the discourse on the more radical nature of current right-wing blocks remains controversial, as we have seen. In primis, the debate about the roots (including a-fascism, neo-fascism, post-fascism) and ideology (populist radical-right, far-right, extreme-right, conservative, even moderate) of the current first party in the coalition and which expresses the PM of Italy, is also controversial. Lately, there has been much debate on the possible process of gradual convergence under the façade of conservativism between radical and extreme-right positions with more 'institutional' and 'moderate-looking' stances, which will keep going. This is plausible, yet a lot will depend on a possible optimal context for right-wing parties: A turn from an external constraint (Diodato, 2014) to an 'external facilitator', e.g., a hypothetical 2024 best scenario for the populist radical-right forces in Europe, based on both the exploit of the ECR at the

EP election and the Republican party victory at the US presidential election, the situation of Italy's public finance will still be in highly precarious waters.

References

Albertazzi, D., and McDonnell, D. (2005). The Lega Nord in the second Berlusconi government: In a league of its own. *West European Politics, 28*(5), 952-972.

Albertazzi, D., and McDonnell, D. (2009). The Parties of the Center Right: Many Oppositions, One Leader. In J. L. Newell (Ed.) *The Italian General Election of 2008: Berlusconi Strikes Back* (pp.102–117). London: Palgrave.

Albertazzi, D., and McDonnell, D. (2010). The Lega Nord back in government. *West European Politics, 33*(6), 1318-1340.

Albertazzi, D., and Newell, J. L. (2015). Introduction: A mountain giving birth to a mouse? On the impact and legacy of Silvio Berlusconi in Italy. *Modern Italy, 20*(1), 3-10.

Albertazzi, D., Giovannini, A., and Seddone, A. (2018). No regionalism please, we are Leghisti! The transformation of the Italian Lega Nord under the leadership of Matteo Salvini. *Regional & Federal Studies, 28*(5), 645-671.

Albertazzi, D., Bonansinga, D., and Zulianello, M. (2021). The right-wing alliance at the time of the Covid-19 pandemic: all change?'. *Contemporary Italian Politics, 13*(2), pp. 181-195.

Berizzi, P. (2021) *E' gradita la camicia nera*. Milano: Rizzoli.

Broder, D. (2023). *Mussolini's Grandchildren: Fascism in Contemporary Italy*. London: Pluto Press.

Bruno, V. A. (2022). "Center-right? What center-right?". Italy's rightwing coalition between Forza Italia's political heritage and the mainstreaming of the far-right. In V.A. Bruno (Ed.) *Populism and Far-right. Trends in Europe* (pp. 163-195). Milan: EduCatt.

Bruno, V. A. (2022b). Online use of Slogans, Symbols and Slurs by the Italian Radical Right. In V. A. Bruno, J.Y. Camus, T. Hof and M. Kreter (Eds.) Symbols & Slogans of the Radical Right Online: Italy, Germany, France (pp. 2-64). ACS.

Bruno, V. A., and Cozzolino, A. (2022). Populism and technocracy during the Covid-19 pandemic in Italy. A two-year balance (2020-2021). In D. Palano (Ed.) *State of Emergency. Italian democracy in times of pandemic* (pp. 153-180). Milan: EduCatt.

Bruno, V. A. and Downes, J. F. (2023). The Radicalisation of the Mainstream: Populist Radical Right Parties and Extreme Right-Wing Movements in Italy (2012-2022). In K. Kondor and M. Littler (Eds.) (pp. 129-144). *The Routledge Handbook of Far-Right Extremism in Europe*. London: Routledge.

Bruno, V. A. and Fazio, F. (2023). Italian governments and political parties vis-à-vis the war in Ukraine. In A. Mihr and C. Pierobon (Eds.), *Polarization, Shifting Borders and Liquid Governance: Studies on Transformation and Development in the OSCE Region* (pp. 265-283). New York: Springer—OSCE Academy in Bishkek (Kyrgyzstan).

Bruno, V. A., J.F. Downes, J. F. and A. Scopelliti (2021). Post-Fascism in Italy: 'So Why This Flame, Mrs. Giorgia Meloni?'. *Culturico*. From https://culturico.com/2021/11/12/post-fascism-in-italy-so-why-this-flame-mrs-giorgia-meloni/.

Castelli Gattinara, P., and Froio, C. (2021). Italy: the Mainstream Right and its Allies, 1994-2018. In T. Bale and C. Rovira Kaltwasser (Eds.) *Riding the Populist Wave. Europe's Mainstream Right in Crisis*. Cambridge: Cambridge University Press, pp. 170-192.

Chiaramonte, A. and De Sio, L. (Eds.) (2024). *Un polo solo. Le elezioni politiche del 2022*. Bologna: Il Mulino.

Coticchia, F. (2015). Effective strategic narratives? Italian public opinion and military operations in Iraq, Libya, and Lebanon. *Italian Political Science Review/Rivista Italiana di Scienza Politica*, 45(1), 53-78.

Coticchia, F. (2021). A sovereignist revolution? Italy's foreign policy under the "Yellow–Green" government. *Comparative European Politics*, 19, 739-759.

Coticchia, F., and S. D'Amato, S. (2018). Can you hear me Major Tom? News, narratives and contemporary military operations: the case of the Italian mission in Afghanistan. *European security*, 27(2), 224-244.

Coticchia, F., and Di Giulio, M. (2023). Nonuse and hypocritical use of strategic narratives in Megaprojects: the case of the Florence high-speed railway. *Policy and Society*, 42(2), 164-183.

Coticchia, F., and Vignoli, V. (2020). Populist parties and foreign policy: The case of Italy's Five Star Movement. *The British Journal of Politics and International Relations*, 22(3), 523-541.

Coticchia, F., and Catanzaro, A. (2022). The fog of words: Assessing the problematic relationship between strategic narratives, (master) frames and ideology. *Media, War & Conflict 15.4 (2022)*: 427-449.

Diodato, E. (2014). *Il vincolo esterno. Le ragioni della debolezza italiana*. Milano: Mimesis.

Donà, A. (2022). The rise of the Radical Right in Italy: the case of Fratelli d'Italia. *Journal of Modern Italian Studies*, 27 (5), 775-794.

Giubilei, F. (2020). *Giorgia Meloni. La rivoluzione dei conservatori*. Roma: Giubilei Regnani.

Griffini, M. (2023). *The Politics of Memory in the Italian Populist Radical Right: From Mare Nostrum to Mare Vostrum*. Oxon: Taylor & Francis.

Ignazi, P. (1994). *L'estrema destra in Europa*. Bologna: Il Mulino.

Invernizzi, M. and Sanuinetti, O. (Eds.) (2023). *Conservatori. Storia e attualità di un pensiero politico*. Milano: Edizioni Ares.

Kelemen, R. D. (2020). The European Union's authoritarian equilibrium. *Journal of European Public Policy*, 27(3), 481-499.

McDonnell, D. (2013). Silvio Berlusconi's personal parties: from Forza Italia to the Popolo Della Liberta. *Political Studies*, 61(1_suppl), 217-233.

Meloni, G. (2021). Io sono Giorgia. *Le mie radici, le mie idee*. Milano: Rizzoli.

Mudde, C. (2004). The Populist Zeitgeist. *Government and Opposition*, 39:4, 541-563.

Mudde, C. (2019). *The far-right today*. Hoboken: John Wiley & Sons.

Mudde, C., and Rovira Kaltwasser, C. (2017). *Populism: A Very Short Introduction*. Oxford: Oxford University Press.

Mueller, S., and Heidelberger, A. (2020). Should we stay or should we join? 30 years of Sovereignism and direct democracy in Switzerland. *European Politics and Society*, 21(2), 182-201.

Newth, G. (2022). Matteo Salvini, Giorgia Meloni, and 'Post-Fascism' as Political Logic. *Political Studies Association Blog*. From https://www.psa.ac.uk/psa/news/matteo-salvini-giorgia-meloni-and-%E2%80%98post-fascism%E2%80%99-political-logic

Newth, G. and Maccaferri, M. (2022). From performative anti-fascism to post-fascism: the Lega (Nord)'s political discourse in historical context. *Journal of Political Ideologies*.

Paolucci, C. (2006). The nature of Forza Italia and the Italian transition. *Journal of Southern Europe and the Balkans*, 8(2), 163-178.

Pasquino, G. (2003). A tale of two parties: Forza Italia and the Left Democrats. *Journal of Modern Italian Studies*, 8(2), 197-215.

Passarelli, G. and Tuorto, D. (2018). *La Lega di Salvini Estrema destra di governo*. Bologna: Il Mulino.

Pirro, A. L. (2023). Far-right: The significance of an umbrella concept. *Nations and Nationalism*, 29(1), 101-112.

Puleo, L. and Piccolino, G. (2022). Back to the post-fascist past or landing in the populist radical right? The brothers of Italy between continuity and change. *South European Society & Politics*, 1–25.

Raniolo, F. (2006). Forza Italia: A leader with a party. *South European society & politics*, 11(3-4), 439-455.

Scopelliti, A. and Bruno, V. A. (2023). Restoration of Sovereignty? Interpretative Lectures of Sovereignism beyond Nationalism and Populism. *Soft Power* 9(2), 191-211.

Tarchi, M. (2003). The Lega Nord. In L. De Winter and H. Tursan (Eds.). *Regionalist parties in Western Europe* (pp. 161–175). London: Routledge.

Vampa, D. (2023). *Brothers of Italy: A New Populist Wave in an Unstable Party System*. Berlini: Springer Nature.

Vassallo, S., and Vignati, R. (2023). *Fratelli di Giorgia. Il partito della destra nazional-conservatrice*. Bologna: Il Mulino.

Verzichelli, L., (2021). Conclusions. The populism-sovereignism linkage: findings, theoretical implications and a new research agenda. In L. Basile and O. Mazzoleni, eds., *Sovereignism and Populism. Citizens, Voters and Parties in Western European Democracies* (108-120). London: Routledge.

Zulianello, M. (2020). Varieties of populist parties and party systems in Europe: from state-of-the-art to the application of a novel classification scheme to 66 parties in 33 countries. *Government and Opposition*, vol. 55 (2), 327–347.

PART TWO
Leading Actors in the Radical-Right Mainstream

Chapter 3
(Northern) League's Case Study: A Text-Based Analysis of Matteo Salvini's Social Media Rhetoric

The (Northern) League is a political party that has always captured much attention from researchers since its foundation. Over the years, scholars have debated the various interpretations they would attribute to this party, such as a federalist party (Mannheimer, 1991; Diamanti, 1995), a regional-populist party (Biorcio, 1991), an ethnoregionalist party (Diamanti and Donaldson, 1997; De Winter, 2003), a radical right party (Gold, 2003; Gómez-Reino Cachafeiro, 2004; Zaslove, 2011) or a soft/hard-Euroskeptic party (Szczerbiak and Taggart, 2008; Quaglia, 2008; Ivaldi et al., 2017). Nevertheless, there is no doubt among these authors about the raison d'être (or founding ideology) behind the building process of the 'Po Valley' party, which is indeed based on the classical cleavage structure of center vs. periphery (or regional cleavage) with the main goal to reclaim independence of the Northern regions from the Italian state. Moreover, although it has recently tried to shift toward a more national identity, the claim for independence (or autonomy) of the Northern regions is still topical at the regional and local levels.

The League's political roots originate from a series of smaller pro-independent parties of the late 1970s and early 1980s (among these, the most important parties were Lega Lombarda, Liga Veneta and Piemònt Autonomista). Consequently, these parties merged into a political coalition named Northern League in 1989, whose main political ideology was to propose regional belonging as the new dominant conflict that would substitute the 'obsolete' conflict of the left vs. right and, therefore, to propose to the Northern Italians a political alternative against the mainstream political forces that were invested by the judicial inquiry on corruption in the early 1990s (the so-called 'mani pulite' inquiry) (Mannheimer, 1991; Diamanti, 1995).

The Northern League has often been associated with studies investigating populist radical right parties (see, e.g., Biorcio, 1997; Kitschelt and McGann, 1997; Albertazzi and McDonnell, 2010). In this sense, the term populist does not refer to the well-established definition conceptualized by Mudde (2004) as a thin ideology between people vs. elites. However, rather, it is understood as a communication strategy employed by the Northern League to deliver its message in the form of a conflict between 'Northern people' versus any type of external enemy. Understandably, for the Northern League's narrative, the central government in Rome that rules the country to the detriment of the Northern Italians (and to the advantage of the Southern Italians) has always been identified as the main 'external' enemy (Biorcio, 1991). In this sense, the League recalls a 'new conflict', but which, in fact, retraces old political and social clashes that have characterized the history of Italy since its foundation (the Italian Risorgimento[37]). In this sense, although based on a classical cleavage, the Northern League has been able to offer its own new collective identity, which appeals to voters from both the left wing and the right wing. The party, therefore, challenges the central government for its inadequacy in solving several issues (such as housing, taxation, health, pensions, services, and crime) and claims to initiate new deregulation processes (similar to the United Kingdom). Ultimately, the main propositions of the Northern League were, thus, to obtain a relative privilege for the people of the North in the redistribution of resources and greater autonomy for the Northern regions (Mannheimer, 1991).

Over the years, the election in 1996 was a decisive moment to the extent that the Northern League addressed its core ideology on federalism. Although strong rhetoric against Southern Italians has

---

[37] The Italian Risorgimento was an historical phenomenon that contributed to the unification of the Italian Kingdom in the XIX century. The building process of this nation has been led by a 'top-down' approach where political elites of the Northern regions (the Kingdom of Sardinia) shaped the unification of all Italian regions through military expansions towards the Southern regions (the Kingdom of the Two Sicilies). Since then, Italy was characterized by a wide north-south divide where on the one hand, the Southern regions claimed to be exploited by the Northern regions and, on the other hand, the Northern regions blamed the Southern regions for their backward economy (Barsotti, 2021).

always characterized the party, the driving force behind the Federalist Project was always justified using an economic rationale. Indeed, the Northern League's claim for the federalist project was driven by the argument that the Southern regions exploited the prosperity of the Northern regions, holding them back from industrial development and economic prosperity (Bull and Gilbert, 2001: 58). Such rhetoric was in addition reinforced alongside the developments of the European integration process (economically and politically). The Northern League would claim in favor of the European Economic Community by arguing that the Northern regions would move on with the other European member states and leave behind the declining economy of the Italian Southern regions (Giordano, 2000). Nevertheless, since the late 1990s, the Northern League has decided to focus on the federalist claim over cultural and ethnic reasons, delivering the message that Northern Italians are a minority ethnic group discriminated against by the rest of the country (Diamanti and Donaldson, 1997; De Winter, 2003).

Consequently, since the early 2000s, the Northern League has fueled its regional identity by driving a new "strategy of politicizing the issue of immigration as a threat to Padanian society[38] and the values of Western society" (Gómez-Reino Cachafeiro, 2004: 140). In this sense, proponents of the radical right interpretation of the Northern League argued that this party strategically "panders to the reactionary and xenophobic instincts" of the electorate (Bull and Gilbert, 2001: 46). Indeed, according to Zaslove (2011: 118), the Northern League employs "what is often referred to as 'differentialist racism', support for ethnic federalism, and opposition to multiculturalism". In line with this point, Gold (2003) put forward the view that the nativist feature of the Northern League has actually been constant since its origin. The only change was by initially addressing the xenophobic discourse against Southern Italian people and, subsequently, shifting the same xenophobic discourse against

---

[38] The Padanian society is often attributed to the citizens living in the Northern regions of Italy including Valle d'Aosta, Piemonte, Lombardia, Trentino Alto Adige, Veneto and Friuli-Venezia Giulia. This attribute was often narrated by the League since its foundation.

immigrants and minority communities such as the Muslim, African and Roman communities.

Finally, in 2018, the Northern League rebranded, moving from a regionalist-oriented party to a national party claiming to represent Italians from all over the country. As such, the party changed its name from Northern League to League in December 2017 (see Figure 4.1). For some authors, this change is an indication that it decided "to abandon its original mission and to de-politicize conflict within the Italian state and to empower the state against the EU" (Caiani and Conti, 2014: 194). Indeed, scholars who vastly investigated the different degrees of Euroskepticism tend to define the League as a soft-Euroskeptic party (see, e.g., Szczerbiak and Taggart, 2008: 134; Quaglia, 2008) or even as a hard-Euroskeptic party (Ivaldi et al., 2017).

Figure 4.1 The development of the League's symbol

From 1989 to 2013   Since December 2017

The League has been able to succeed and survive in the last forty years (it is, currently, the oldest party in the Italian party system). Figure 4.2 shows the electoral performances of the League from 1983 to 2019 in national and European elections. From this figure, we can observe that the League did not experience significant electoral successes in the 1980s. Nevertheless, from 1992 to 2014, the League was a relevant political competitor in Italy, experiencing constant ups and downs. Over the years, the League has been able to access several governmental coalitions and to hold numerous ministries. The League supported the Berlusconi governments four times (1994, 2001, 2005 and 2011), the first Conte government (2018), the following Draghi's government (2020), and, finally, the first Meloni government (2023). In some of the more recent elections, both at the national (2018) and the European (2019) levels, the League experienced impressive electoral performances. Indeed, thanks to the 2018 national election, the League succeeded in winning the leadership within the right-wing coalition against the Brothers of Italy (FdI) and Italy Forward (FI). While, in the 2019 European election, the League was also the most electorally successful party in Italy and the most successful radical right party at the European level (when considering the Western European countries). Eventually, in the 2022 general election, the League had a considerable electoral decrease and lost supremacy as the first party in the right-wing coalition, shifting Matteo Salvini's leadership of the right-wing coalition to that of Giorgia Meloni from Brothers of Italy.

Figure 4.2 The League's electoral performances from 1983 to 2022 in percentages

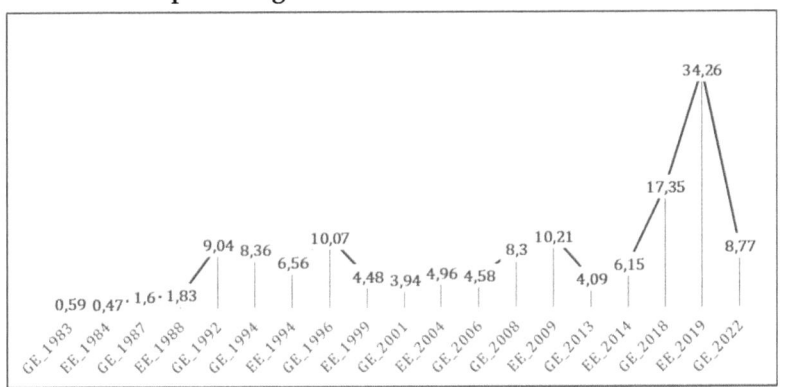

Source: Author's elaboration from Ministero dell'Interno data (2021). Notes: GE: General Election, EE: European Election

As the League grew year after year, capturing the attention of many scholars about its narratives, political offers and impact on Italian and European party politics, in this chapter, we are interested in exploring Matteo Salvini's social media rhetoric delivered on Twitter (Now X) in the last decade. As such, focusing on his Twitter official account, we will explore tweets labeled with some of the ideologies that are often associated with populist radical right parties (populism, nativism, authoritarianism, religion, souverainisme) and its core ideological foundation (federalism) through an automated text analysis approach. This chapter will be developed as follows. It will first review Matteo Salvini's political career and leadership within the League to provide a comprehensive understanding of his pivotal role within the party. As the reader will notice, the League (and Matteo Salvini's personal political experience) faced multiple periods of incumbency and opposition. Such experience will be the driving pull of our research questions' chapter. Second, we will briefly explain the data collected for this analysis and the methods applied. The third part will be dedicated to presenting the main results of this analysis and answering the research questions. Finally, the last section of this chapter will provide our conclusive thoughts on Matteo Salvini's social media rhetoric on Twitter and its implications for the current Italian political landscape.

Matteo Salvini's political profile

Matteo Salvini is one of the most prominent politicians within the current Italian political system, especially in the last decade. Starting from the bottom, Salvini joined the Northern League in the early 1990s and quickly rose through the ranks, becoming the secretary of the Movimento Giovani Padani (League's Youth Movement) and being elected as city councillor of Milan. After a local political experience in the city council of Milan and a brief journalistic career as a reporter for the newspaper *La Padania* (the Po Valley) and director of the radio station Radio Padania Libera (The Po Valley Free Radio), he was elected as an MEP from 2004 to 2006 gaining more national (and European) visibility. Salvini's controversial political communication strategy, focused on xenophobic and federalist ideals, garnered him even more attention, which characterized the shift of the Northern League's communication strategy in 1996. In the following years, Salvini continued to be elected to higher offices in the following electoral events, shifting his institutional role from city councillor of Milan in 2006 to MP in the Chamber of Deputies in 2008 and, eventually, EMP in 2009. This last electoral success was a turning point in his career, as it propelled him into the national spotlight. Eventually, the culmination of the political rise within the Northern League was his nomination as secretary (and leader) of the party, challenging the incumbent leader, Roberto Maroni. In 2013, Matteo Salvini won the leadership election with 82% of the vote, and he immediately set about implementing his vision for the party.

Since then, Salvini reshaped the Northern League political agenda, transforming the party into a more populist and nationalist party with a focus on anti-immigration policies and Euroskepticism. A few days after his election, Salvini published an article in *La Padania* that showed the new path of the party:

> "Internationally, the priority is to crumble this euro and refound this Europe. Yes, therefore, to alliances even with the only ones who are not eurofools: the French of Le Pen, the Dutch of Wilders, the Austrians of Molzer, the Finns [...]in short, with those of the Europe of homelands"[39] (*La Padania*, 2013).

As such, under Salvini's leadership, the Northern League shifted its focus from regionalism to national issues, particularly on migration and European issues. The party subsequently embraced even more emphatic populist rhetoric with the aim of defending the needs and the rights of the 'forgotten' Italians who were left behind by the national and transnational establishments (often identified through the Italian left-wing and the EU). In the 2014 European Parliament election, Salvini was elected as MEP, becoming a prominent figure of the souverainist sphere within the European Parliament group of Europe Freedom and Democracy (EFD). He became a vocal critic of the EU's immigration policies, arguing that they were encouraging illegal immigration and threatening the security of European

---

[39] Here the original version translates from Italian: "A livello internazionale la priorità è sgretolare questo euro e rifondare questa Europea. Sì, quindi, alle alleanze anche con gli unici che non sono europirla: i francesi della Le Pen, gli olandesi di Wilders, gli austriaci di Molzer, i finlandesi...insomma, con quelli dell'Europa delle patrie".

countries. He also called for Italy to leave the eurozone, stating that the common currency was damaging the Italian economy.

In the 2018 electoral campaign, Salvini reshaped the party to his own leadership's interests, changing the name of the party from Northern League to League Salvini Premier and going beyond the Po Valley secessionism that has characterized the party since its foundation. Eventually, after gaining the leadership of the right-wing coalition in 2018, he even formed a coalition with the Five Star Movement, forming, for the very first time, the most populist and Euroskeptic government in the Italian Republic's history: the first Conte cabinet (Natale, 2018). On this occasion, Salvini was appointed as the deputy prime minister and minister of the interior in the new government. However, after a series of political disputes with the Five Stars Movement, Salvini left the Conte government. Subsequently, the Five Stars Movement coalited with the Democratic Party to form the second Conte government, which relegated the League, again, to the opposition. This period in opposition did not last long; in fact, after a worsening of the COVID-19 pandemic in Italy, Mario Draghi (the former president of the European Central Bank) was clamored at by the parties in the Italian Parliament (excluding Brothers of Italy) to revive the country.

Moreover, on this occasion, members of the League were called back to public office. Since then, the League has held and still holds (after the 2022 general elections) institutional roles. However, Salvini is currently challenged by the rise of the new Giorgia Meloni's leadership within the right-wing coalition.

Matteo Salvini's political career has involved both periods of incumbency and opposition. As such, the opportunity to analyze Salvini's social media rhetoric gives us the opportunity to test whether politicians tend to deliver less polarizing rhetoric in times of incumbency. The third wave of the radical right literature already confirmed that populist radical right parties and leaders tend to moderate their positions when holding governmental roles (see, for example, Bernhard, 2020; Borbáth and Gessler, 2023). However, this chapter aims to test this assumption by comparing Salvini's social media rhetoric on Twitter in both periods of incumbency and opposition. For this reason, we want to answer the following research question: *how did Salvini's social media rhetoric evolve in times of incumbency and opposition?*

Data and methods

Twitter data

This chapter's analysis will be based on the social media narrative delivered by Salvini. Among the different social media platforms, we argue that Twitter still plays a fundamental role as a communicative tool that gives consent to politicians to bypass the mainstream media and to directly communicate with their electorate without any filter or delegations from third entities (Stier et al. 2018). The recent literature on populist radical right additionally insists on the pivotal role of the leaders' accounts of this kind of political party who not only represent such political movements but also shape political parties' goals and agenda — see the case of Donald Trump with the Republican Party in the United States or Viktor Orbán and the party Fidesz in Hungary. Accordingly, we draw on multiple studies that have already demonstrated that Matteo Salvini's Twitter account is a reliable source to explore the political narrative of the leader as his principal communicative instrument to his electorate (or followers) (see, e.g., Berti and Loner, 2021). Therefore, for our analyzes, we exclusively collected data from the official Twitter account of Salvini named "@matteosalvinimi". The time frame that we included for this analysis starts from the first tweets published by the politician to the most recent date once we started collecting data: from March 23, 2011, through March 6, 2023. This time frame is ideal to answer our research question for two main reasons. First, it gives us the opportunity to analyze an extended period that involves all his Twitter experience, providing a holistic overview of Salvini's social media rhetoric. Second, for a more practical reason, it allows us to explore the social media narrative of Matteo Salvini both in times of incumbency and opposition (twice).

Data preparation and methods

To capture Matteo Salvini's tweets, we used RStudio and the AcademicTwitteR library (Barrie and Chun-ting 2021). We accessed the historical archive of data published on Twitter using a Twitter Academic API and collected all tweets and retweets published in the query. We collected 52,682 tweets. We then employed various pre-processing techniques, such as cleaning steps for texts as data. For this phase, we combined both the dplyr package (Wickham et al. 2022) and the tm package in R (Feinerer and Hornik 2020). We removed all meaningless features such as URL/HTML and emojis. We also eliminated Italian language-specific features (e.g., apostrophes). We lowercased all the words in our data to ensure that the same words would be counted together. We removed predefined stop words, punctuation, and unwanted white space. However, we did not stem or lemmatize words.[40] Alternatively, some words have been merged with an underscore to allow the counting of concepts that would eventually be missing (see the dictionaries in Table 4.1). Eventually, to perform statistical analyzes, we converted our dataset (with the cleaned texts) into a document feature matrix through the Quanteda package (Benoit et al. 2018). In this new format, the matrix was structured with texts in rows and features in columns.

Once the data preparation was complete, we implemented two analytical approaches to answer the research question of this chapter. For the first part of the analysis, we categorized tweets employing a dictionary-based approach (Reveilhac and Morselli, 2022). After we assigned lists of keywords that represent the six League's ideological discourses, each tweet was then scanned by the computer and categorized with a label to its referring ideology, whether one of the keywords was present in its text. This first step allows us to identify the tweets that shall be analyzed.

---

[40] This step was not necessary thanks to some of the features provided by the Quanteda package that allows the identification of stemmed words even when the whole corpus is not stemmed as well.

Table 4.1 Dictionaries

Authoritarianism dictionary		Nativist dictionary	
Italian terms	English translation	Italian terms	English translation
"sicurezza"	"security"	"razza"	"race"
"guardia_finanza"	"financial_guard"	"migrante"	"migrant"
"polizia"	"police"	"africa"	"africa"
"carabbinier*"	"carabbinier*"	"sbarchi"	"landings"
"forze_ordine"	"law_forces"	"openarms"	"openarms"
"forze_armate"	"armed_forces"	"immigrato"	"immigrant"
Federalism dictionary		"confini"	"borders"
Italian terms	English translation	"profugo"	"refugee"
"federal*"	"federal*"	"moschea"	"mosque"
"autonomi*"	"autonomous*"	"clandestino"	"clandestine"
"padania"	"padania"	"fondamentalismo"	"fundamentalism"
"region*"	"region*"	"integralista"	"fundamentalist"
"provinc*"	"provinc*"	"poligamia"	"polygamy"
Populist dictionary		"sharia"	"sharia"
Italian terms	English translation	"islam"	"Islam"
"antidemocratic*"	"undemocratic*"	"occidente"	"western"
"casta"	"caste"	"gaza"	"gaza"
"consens*"	"consens*"	"hamas"	"hamas"
"corrot*"	"corrot*"	"maometto"	"Mohammed"
"disonest*"	"dishonest"	"arabo"	"Arab"
"elit*"	"elit*"	"musulmano"	"Muslim"
"establishment"	"establishment"	"straniero"	"foreigner"
"ingann*"	"ingann*"	"qatar"	"qatar"
"mentir*"	"lie*"	"irregolare"	"irregular"
"menzogn*"	"lizogn*"	"porti"	"ports"
"partitocrazia"	"partitocracy"	"iusscholae"	"iusscholae"
		"iussoli"	"iussoli"
		Religious dictionary	
		Italian terms	English translation

"propagand*"	"propagand*"	"vaticano"	"vatican"
"scandal*"	"scandal*"	"papa"	"pope"
"tradim*"	"tradim*"	"bergoglio"	"bergoglio"
"tradir*"	"tradir*"	"ratzinger"	"ratzinger"
"tradit*"	"tradit*"	"pontifex"	"pontifex"
"vergogn*"	"shame"	"chiesa"	"church"
"verità"	"truth"	"cattolico"	"catholic"
"abitant*"	"abitant*"	"religione"	"religion"
"cittadin*"	"citizen*"	"bibbia"	"bible"
"consummator*"	"consumer*"	"vangelo"	"gospel"
	"taxpayer*"	"gesù"	"jesus"
"contribuent*"	"elector*"	"fede"	"faith"
"elettor*"	"people"	"cristo"	"christ"
"gente"	"people"	"vergine"	"virgin"
"popol*"		"laico"	"lay"

European dictionary		"parrocchia"	"parish"
Italian terms	English translation	"cristiano"	"Christian"
		"divino"	"divine"
"unione_europea"	"european_union"	"catechismo"	"catechism"
"ue"	"eu"	"dio"	"god"
"euro"	"euro"		
"commissione_europea"	"european_commission"		
"burocrati"	"bureaucrats"		
"bruxelles"	"brussels"		
"sovrani*"	"souvrain*"		

To explore how Salvini's social media rhetoric has changed over the years, we will compare the tweets' distribution associated with ideological discourses from March 2011 to March 2023. This visualization will provide straightforward insights into whether his communication strategy has changed over time in terms of emphasis. The second method will be a top-words frequency analysis through word clouds. Each word cloud will show every ideological discourse by comparing times of incumbency and not. The reason for using this method is twofold. First, it allows us to observe which most frequent features (or concepts) are more relevant within each ideological discourse. Second, such a technique of visualization allows a straightforward and intuitive method to observe whether ideological discourses exclusively deliver their domains or if other ideological discourses crosscut them.

Radical right mobilization on Salvini's social media rhetoric

The chronological distribution of all collected and selected tweets through the six dictionaries over the years observed (Figure 4.3) generally shows different results as regards the relevance of one ideological discourse to the other. Among the six different ideological discourses used in Salvini's Twitter account, the nativist, authoritarian, populist and Euroskeptic discourses are the most frequently employed, while the religious and the federalist discourses are the least. Starting with the religious one, the relative insignificance of the religious discourse compared to the other ideologies is somewhat surprising given that Salvini is often associated with religious themes such as defending the 'traditional' or 'natural' family composed of a mother and a father, rejecting the 'womb for rent' (surrogate pregnancy) or same-sex marriage, and adoptions (Donà, 2020). However, it is important to distinguish between a religious or ultraconservative position and an anti-LGBT position. The examples mentioned above do not explicitly refer to religious topics and could actually be categorized as anti-LGBT narratives. As such, Salvini (and the League) may use religious topics as a proxy to deliver anti-LGBT narratives. For that reason, to avoid mis-categorizing tweets that do not really address the religious discourse but an anti-LGBT discourse, we used a more restrictive religious dictionary, explaining, despite Salvini's association with religious themes, why his Twitter account employs the religious discourse the least in this analysis. Even Matteo Salvini's federalist discourse irrelevance is not a surprising result. He has always advocated for more regional federalism as a goal within the League's political agenda, but he never pushed for real autonomy in the Northern regions. Instead, Salvini transformed the League's interest into that of a national party that focused on the interests of all Italians rather than just Northern citizens (Caiani and Conti, 2014).

The second element we want to highlight is the tendency of the other four ideological discourses (nativism, authoritarianism, populism, and Euroskepticism). Overall, all these ideological discourses have shown a tendency to increase in salience since Salvini's social media rhetoric of the early years, peaking when the League joined the first Conte government in 2018. What is even more interesting is that these saliences do not decrease after joining the government but rather increase during the period of incumbency. This is consistent with our expectations that leaders representing populist radical right values will keep similar levels of salience to address their usual narratives on social media or even increase the salience of these topics during their time in office.

Finally, another point to note from Figure 4.3 is a contradictory tendency observed after the League left the first Conte cabinet. All four ideological discourses showed a significant decrease during the period of opposition. Interestingly, the fall in salience did not occur immediately after the fall of the first Conte cabinet but was consistently high until January 2020. The decline began when the COVID-19 pandemic hit Italy between February and March 2020. This suggests that the global pandemic could have influenced Salvini's social media rhetoric, causing a significant decrease in the salience of every ideological discourse during the crisis. Moreover, this trend continued even when the League joined the Draghi cabinet, a technical government, and later the Meloni cabinet, a political government. The decrease in salience observed during the period of opposition suggests that external events and political context influence Salvini's rhetoric, and such conditions contradict our expectations that populist radical right leaders keep similar communication strategies despite being in government or opposition.

Figure 4.3 Distribution of ideological discourses within Matteo Salvini's Twitter account on a yearly basis

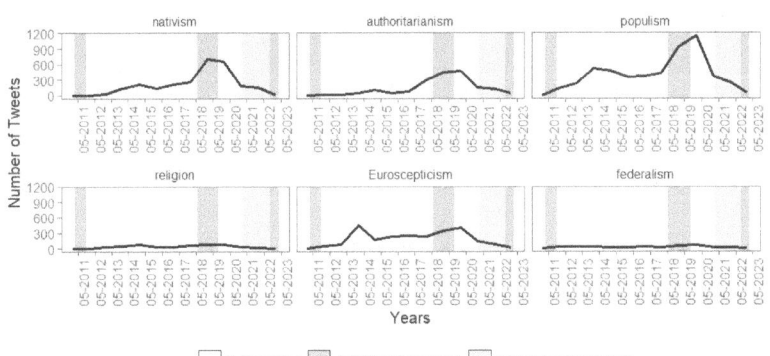

Given the contradictory results from the previous figure, to understand the above analysis better and especially the implications of the last period observed (once COVID-19 hit Italy), we now introduce Figure 4.4, which provides the same topics observed in Figure 4.3, but on a monthly basis and electoral events. This allows us to see with more detail whether the observable peaks' time location coincides with such significant electoral events. Figure 4.4 examines the monthly distribution of ideological discourses on Matteo Salvini's Twitter account. It provides a detailed observation of how much his rhetoric fluctuated around electoral events, whether Salvini was in incumbency or in opposition periods.[41]

---

[41] The following dates are the electoral events we took into account: 24th February 2013 (national election), 22nd and 25th May 2014 (European election), 11th June 2017 (local election), 4th March 2018 (national election), 26th May 2019 (European election), 25th September 2022 (national election).

Figure 4.4 Distribution of ideological discourses within Matteo Salvini's Twitter account on a monthly basis

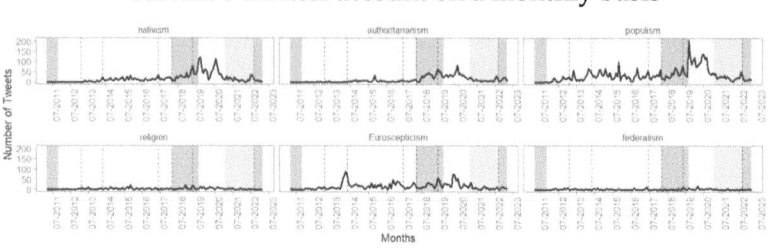

As we expected, Matteo Salvini's social media rhetoric is observed to coincide with electoral events. This is not surprising as it is quite reasonable that a politician tends to share topics (and, therefore, ideas) especially in times of electoral campaign. However, the six topics identified within Salvini's tweets are approached differently. The topics of nativism, populism, and Euroskepticism are much more responsive to these electoral events. Religion and federalism do completely ignore electoral events, while authoritarianism shows peaks during (few) electoral events, but it is also employed even in periods between elections.

It is interesting to observe that the authoritarian discourse did not start to increase in times of opposition, but rather, it significantly developed in times of incumbency, more specifically after the creation of the first Conte government. As presented in the previous section, Matteo Salvini was appointed as deputy prime minister and minister of the interior. Especially for the latter, Salvini is mostly remembered for spreading a political campaign focused on law and order and anti-immigration. In order to combat both phenomena, the 'giallo-verde' government[42] enacted Salvini's Security Decrees, which, among others, mostly included the following measures: reduction in the number of asylum seekers, strengthening of border controls, strengthening of expulsion policies and introduction of urban security, providing a series of measures to

---

[42] It means 'yellow-green' government. This was the metaphor assigned to describe the coalition between the Five Stars Movement and the League.

ensure greater security in cities, including the reinforcement of the police force and the introduction of the 'urban Daspo' for violent behavior in stadiums and high-traffic areas, discouraging forms of protest and street demonstrations.

On the other hand, while focusing on nativism, populism and Euroskepticism, Figure 4.4 shows how Salvini tailors his messaging to appeal to his audience, especially during electoral campaigns. For instance, the Euroskeptic discourse coincides heavily with electoral events, particularly the 2014 and 2019 European elections. Eventually, this discourse has again re-emerged with the onset of the COVID-19 pandemic, while Salvini has accused the EC (and the Italian government) of mismanagement during the vaccination campaign. Similarly, the nativist and populist discourses reached new peaks in times of opposition, but they drastically decreased once the League joined Draghi's government (as mentioned above).

However, if we zoom in on the timeframe since February 2021 (see Figure 4.5) and analyze the three most used ideological discourses (nativism, authoritarianism and populism), two contrasting tendencies become apparent. In Draghi's cabinet, Salvini's Twitter account has reduced the number of tweets on these three ideological discourses. In fact, when the League joined Mario Draghi's technical government, there was a perceived 'moderation' of Salvini's social media rhetoric due to the Italian government's responsibility to act properly in the face of the COVID-19 pandemic (and, lately, with the war in Ukraine). One should also notice that such a decrease is in line with the overall social media strategy of Salvini. Figure 4.6 shows that the overall number of tweets dramatically decreased a few months after the advent of COVID-19 in Italy especially with the start of the war in Ukraine. However, during the electoral campaign for the 2022 general elections, there were several spikes, albeit lighter than during the first Conte government. These spikes confirmed Salvini's tendency to increase (even if slightly) populist radical right ideological discourses on his Twitter account, regardless of being in government; what is even more interesting is the period after joining Meloni's government. All three discourses show a low level of salience when compared to the previous months. However, one should also notice that authoritarianism and populism still present peak moments while nativism is decreasing.

On the one hand, the increase in the salience of the authoritarian and populist discourses can be explained by the first bills proposed by Meloni's cabinet against rave parties, which punish the invasion of land or public or private buildings by groups of more than 50 people in a context that may represent a danger to public order, public safety, or public health. Penalties for those who organize these illegal rallies are as follows: from three to six years imprisonment for the organizers and fines of up to ten thousand euros. On the other hand, the nativist discourse decreased after the first months within Meloni's government. This can be explained by the impossibility of the League to operate as an 'external' party within its own majority. This political strategy was already employed during the first Conte cabinet, blaming the Five Stars Movement for its inefficiency in handling the immigration issue (Scopelliti, 2020). Within Meloni's cabinet, such communication strategy cannot be employed as the League now belongs to a majority that is ideologically aligned to its populist radical right-wing ideals, including anti-immigration sentiments.

Figure 4.5 Distribution of nativism and populism within Matteo Salvini's Twitter account from 02/2021 to 03/2023

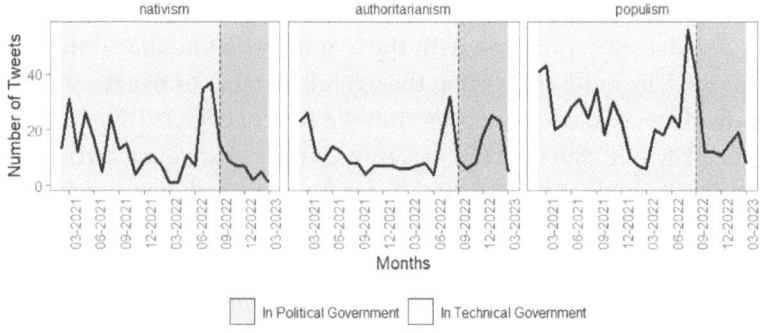

Figure 4.6 Distribution of total tweets within Matteo Salvini's Twitter account on a monthly basis

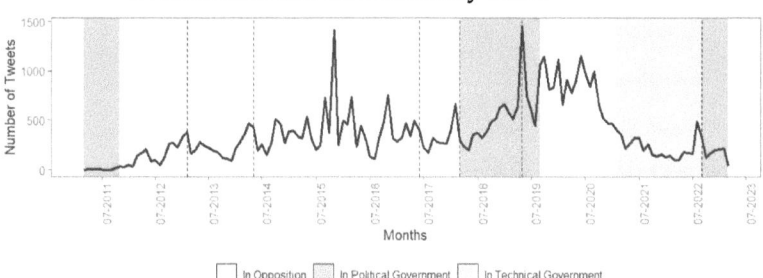

A "frozen" social media rhetoric?

In this section, we will compare word clouds representing the six ideological discourses delivered by Salvini's Twitter account. Each word cloud represents one specific ideological discourse, and it shows the most frequent words employed by tweets when published in times of incumbency and in times of opposition.

Figure 4.6 Word clouds of the nativist discourse compared in times of incumbency and opposition

Starting with the nativist tweets, it is evident that the two-word clouds display both similarities and differences. Immigration is the overarching topic that appears in both word clouds. The 'in opposition' word cloud often refers to clandestine immigration, landings, Lampedusa, and control. It even features the hashtag '#governoclandestino' (clandestine government), which accuses the left-wing government, led by Matteo Renzi at the time, of facilitating rising migratory flows into Italy. Such a narrative was even employed after the League left the first Conte cabinet.

"At #Christmas we are all better, but no more fools! #clandestine government #votosubito"[43] (@matteosalvinimi, 2016).

" ● We are ready to give battle, inside and outside Parliament, to stop the Ius Soli and prevent the Security Decrees from being changed. #governmentclandestine"[44] (@matteosalvinimi, 2019).

Focusing on the 'in government' word cloud, when Matteo Salvini joined the government in 2018, this narrative remained unchanged. Nevertheless, the focus shifted to other keywords that highlight the effectiveness of the yellow-green government in keeping ports closed to migrants and asylum seekers, as seen in '#portichiusi'. This policy leads, according to Salvini's account, to a significant decrease in deaths (morti) in the Mediterranean Sea, as indicated by the term 'less' (meno). Moreover, the word cloud includes the names of various ships that received media attention during that time, including those belonging to NGOs, such as *Aquarius* and *Open Arms*, and the Italian safeguard ship *Diciotti*.

" ● Ship Open Arms, Ong and Spanish flagged, collected 200 immigrants, asks for an Italian port after Malta's refusal (which landed, rightly, a woman and a child). Italian ports are CLOSED! For the human traffickers and those who help them, the fun is over"[45] (@matteosalvinimi, 2018).

Despite the similarities between the two-word clouds, the 'in opposition' cloud also presents another narrative. This often links the immigration phenomenon with 'Islam' and 'ius soli'. Notably, during times of opposition, the populist radical right tends to emphasize this theme, underscoring the dichotomous conflict between 'us' (Italians) and 'them' (immigrants), who are deemed culturally incompatible with Italy.

---

[43] The original tweet: A #Natale siamo tutti più buoni, ma non più fessi! #governoclandestino #votosubito https://t.co/dYjfEeYiQX.
[44] The original tweet: ● Siamo pronti a dare battaglia, dentro e fuori il Parlamento, per fermare lo Ius Soli ed evitare che si cambino i Decreti Sicurezza. #governoclandestino https://t.co/I5SLmh1Pc9.
[45] The original text: ● Nave Open Arms, Ong e bandiera spagnola, ha raccolto 200 immigrati, chiede un porto italiano dopo il rifiuto di Malta (che ha sbarcato, giustamente, una donna e un bambino). I porti italiani sono CHIUSI! Per i trafficanti di esseri umani e per chi li aiuta, la pacchia è finita.

90   THE RISE OF THE RADICAL RIGHT IN ITALY

"A MOSQUE in Milan? Maybe in the next Century [...] As long as a certain kind of Islam continues to mean [...]"[46] (@matteosalvinimi, 2012).

"'Islamic TERRORISTS on INFLATABLE BOATS left Tunisia', Palermo Prosecutor's Office investigates and arrests 15 people".[47] (@matteosalvinimi, 2017).

"There are thousands of Islamic terrorists in Libya: the risk of infiltration on the boats is a certainty. This is why FIRMNESS is needed, to reiterate that no one is landing in Italy".[48] (@matteosalvinimi, 2019).

Figure 4.7 Word clouds of the authoritarian discourse compared in times of incumbency and opposition

---

[46] The original text: Una MOSCHEA a Milano? Magari nel prossimo Secolo [...] Fino a che un certo tipo di Islam continuerà a significare [...] http://t.co/kuvXuRPdhF.

[47] The original text: "TERRORISTI islamici sui GOMMONI partiti dalla Tunisia", la Procura di Palermo indaga e ferma 15 persone. https://t.co/NAkxkswuMc.

[48] The original text: In Libia ci sono migliaia di terroristi islamici: il rischio di infiltrazioni sui barconi è una certezza. Per questo serve FERMEZZA, ribadire che in Italia non si sbarca. https://t.co/xAPKfHOILm.

When examining the authoritarian tweets, differences are noticeable. Both word clouds mostly refer to law enforcement officers responsible for security in cities, such as 'polizia', 'carabinieri', and 'polizia penitenziaria', underlying the League's support for these institutions. However, the 'in government' word cloud also emphasizes the immigration issue with order and drug dealers (see 'ordine' and 'spacciatori'), associating immigrants as an issue that might destabilize Italian society, and for that reason, they must be deported (see 'espulso'). As such, the 'in government' word cloud highlights the League's efficiency in handling immigration issues. It often employed the expression 'finita la pacchia' (the fun is over) associated with the negligence of the left-wing governments and the migrants' blame for taking advantage of the 'generous' Italian integration policies.

> "#Salvini on #decretosalvini: asylum seekers who commit crimes will have their asylum applications suspended. Those who commit crimes will be EXPULSED. #Mattino5"[49] (@matteosalvinimi, 2018).

There is also a reference to fighting terrorism (without specifying the type) and the mafia (e.g., '#lamafiafaschifo'). On the other hand, within the 'in opposition' word cloud, Salvini accuses the left-wing party that wants to cancel Salvini's Security Decrees. Overall, both word clouds share similarities in their support of law enforcement officers. However, the 'in government' cloud also emphasizes the link between immigration and the disruption of societal order. Additionally, it underscores the League's effectiveness in handling issues related to immigration, terrorism, and the mafia.

> "#Salvini: I don't look at the polls, as a minister I am operational 24 hours a day. Today we returned to the community 491 properties, seized from the mafia, scattered around Lazio. #ariachetirala7 @ariachetira #lamafiamifaschifo"[50] (@matteosalvinimi, 2018).

---

[49] The original text: #Salvini su #decretosalvini: ai richiedenti asilo che delinquono verrà sospesa la domanda di asilo. Chi commette reati verrà ESPULSO. #Mattino5 (@matteosalvinimi, 2018).

[50] The original text: #Salvini: Non guardo i sondaggi, da ministro sono operativo 24 ore su 24. Oggi abbiamo restituito alla collettività 491 immobili, sequestrati

Figure 4.8 Word clouds of the populist discourse compared in times of incumbency and opposition

The populist tweets highlight a significant difference in how the populist discourse is utilized during times of incumbency and opposition. While in government, tweets categorized as populist do not focus on specific topics but instead cut across multiple domains. These tweets criticize the left wing, law and order, elections, the citizenship salary (while in coalition with the Five Stars Movement), economics, immigration, and even foreign politics. On the other hand, the 'in opposition' word cloud demonstrates a more coherent communication strategy when employing a populist discourse. Salvini's tweets often use keywords that resonate with the people,

---

alla mafia, sparsi in giro per il Lazio. #ariachetirala7 @ariachetira #lamafiamifaschifo.

such as 'gente', 'popolo', and 'cittadini', underscoring Salvini's proximity to his electorate. The second distinguishable element is the presence of a significant number of words that evoke 'negative' sentiments often associated with populist discourses, such as traitors, treason, shame, and Italian pride: all keywords that recall the ideological dichotomy between the elite versus the people underlying the treason of the elites for not taking care of the interests of the people.

> "I am listening to LETTA on Rai Tre by Lucia Annunziata. A pain. A disgrace. A nothingness. The emptiness. The rhetoric [...]"[51]
> (@matteosalvinimi, 2013).
> "#Renzi is against the suspension of #Schengen and border control. Renzi is complicit in the INVASION, Renzi is a traitor. #Salvini"[52]
> (@matteosalvinimi, 2016).
> "You should be ashamed, you are ruining the most beautiful country, importing fake refugees and Covid positives, day and night: the judgement of the Italians will be without appeal. #clandestine government"[53]
> (@matteosalvinimi, 2020).

---

[51] The original text: Sto ascoltando LETTA su Rai Tre da Lucia Annunziata. Una pena. Una vergogna. Il nulla. Il vuoto. La retorica [...]. http://t.co/7aU6yFNDB3.
[52] The original text: #Renzi è contrario alla sospensione di #Schengen e al controllo dei confini. Renzi è complice dell'INVASIONE, Renzi è un traditore. #Salvini.
[53] The original text: Dovete vergognarvi, state rovinando il Paese più bello, importando finti profughi e positivi al Covid, giorno e notte: il giudizio degli italiani sarà senza appello. #governoclandestino.

Figure 4.9 Word clouds of the religious discourse compared in times of incumbency and opposition

Salvini's social media rhetoric on religious tweets varies depending on whether the League is in government or opposition. In his 'in government' tweets, he often mentions the expression of someone (see 'qualcuno'). An (external) actor that can cover an undefined umbrella of 'others' (thus, enemies) shifting from elitist leadership culturally far from the people or someone who does not belong to the same cultural Catholic background, thus referring to foreigners. These expressions are frequently associated with Catholic religious symbols like faith, Catholicism, Jesus, and the crib.

> "Nativity scene 'of the immigrants' in Milan, with an inflatable boat instead of a manger to protest against #DecretoSalvini. Authors? The usual 'kompagni' (who, if it goes well, have never made a Nativity scene at home in

their lives). I don't know whether to laugh or cry, I'll limit myself to a: #vivailChristmas!"⁵⁴ (@salvenimi, 2018).

In contrast, Salvini's 'in opposition' tweets often refer to two main religious topics: Pope Giovanni Paolo II and God. Salvini cites Pope Giovanni Paolo II to associate with Catholic institutions while distancing himself from Pope Francesco, whom he considers too reformist for Italian ultraconservative movements. Second, Salvini often refers to God while sharing tweets and prayers following serious news events or natural disasters that have occurred in Italy or concern Italian victims in general. However, such keywords are also used to deliver another topic characteristic of religious tweets when in opposition, which is the immigration issue. It is noteworthy that the immigration issue is highly prevalent in these tweets, with keywords such as Islam, citizenship, stop invasions, refugees, and Lampedusa. This indicates that the religious domain is not a core ideology of Salvini's social media rhetoric, but it rather serves as a tool to convey anti-immigration sentiments.

> "#Salvini: If it bothers you the crucifix, the nativity scene, our traditions, GO HOME! #Pontida17"⁵⁵ (@salvenimi, 2017).

---

54 The original text: Presepe 'degli immigrati' a Milano, con un gommone al posto della mangiatoia per protestare contro #DecretoSalvini. Autori? I soliti 'kompagni' (che, se va bene, il Presepe in casa non l'hanno mai fatto in vita loro). Non so se ridere o piangere, mi limiterò a un: #vivailNatale! https://t.co/eJKuielbOC.
55 The original text: #Salvini: Se ti dà fastidio il crocefisso, il presepe, le nostre tradizioni, TORNA A CASA TUA! #Pontida17.

Figure 4.10 Word clouds of the Euroskeptic discourse compared in times of incumbency and opposition

Moving to the Euroskeptic discourse, the 'in government' word cloud covers multiple topics that address the inefficiency and distance of the EU. Salvini addresses these issues in his social media rhetoric. However, he does not use them to address other narratives of the League's political agenda, whereas the 'in opposition' word cloud heavily focuses on hard-Euroskeptic topics, more specifically, the uselessness of the single European currency. Starting with Salvini's 'in government' tweets, as stated before, no dominant topic is addressed. However, he specifically targets the EU, and the EC is often his interlocutor. He frequently refers to terms that criticize the inefficiency and distance of the EU, using words like European bureaucracy, bureaucrats, and bankers.

> "Do the words and threats of Juncker and other European bureaucrats continue to drive up the spread, with the aim of attacking the Italian government and economy? We are ready to ask for damages from those who want to harm Italy".[56] (@matteosalvinimi, 2018).

The 'in opposition' tweets, on the other hand, focus heavily on keywords against the European common currency, like euro, currency, '#bastaeuro' (#enough euro), and Bruxelles. It is essential to note that while Salvini addresses the EU's inefficiency in his 'in government' tweets, he does not necessarily advocate leaving the EU or the common European currency. Instead, he focuses on the need for reform within the organization. In contrast, the 'in opposition' tweets primarily advocate leaving the EU and abandoning the common currency to regain national sovereignty.

> "We will be part of a group of over 100 MEPs who want to DISMANTLE THIS EUROPE. Out of the EURO the WORK starts again! #bastaeuro @Rainews24"[57] (#matteosalvinimi, 2014).

---

[56] The original text: Le parole e le minacce di Juncker e di altri burocrati europei continuano a far salire lo spread, con l'obiettivo di attaccare il governo e l'economia italiane? Siamo pronti a chiedere i danni a chi vuole il male dell'Italia. https://t.co/QFPAKMwFew.

[57] Teh original text: Saremo parte di gruppo di oltre 100 deputati che vogliono SMONTARE QUESTA EUROPA. Fuori dall'EURO il LAVORO riparte! #bastaeuro @Rainews24.

Figure 4.11 Word clouds of the federalist discourse compared in times of incumbency and opposition

Salvini's federalist discourse appears coherent in both government and opposition, although it is delivered through two different approaches. In the 'in government' tweets, the concept of autonomy is predominant, but other topics such as authoritarian discourses (e.g., security, justice), economy (e.g., flat tax, citizenship salary, pensions) and immigration are also addressed. In fact, Salvini does not provide specific goals or achievements related to regional autonomy but instead includes it in a bullet point list to communicate the government's priorities to his electorate, particularly for the League.

"I feel like sharing my joy with you! Jobs, less taxes, immigration, fiscal peace, pensions, autonomy, security: from words to deeds! ● LIVE > https://t.co/Th3j3Sppxf"[58] (@matteosalvinimi, 2018).

In contrast, the 'in opposition' tweets focus on keywords that recall the Po Valley secessionist spirit, such as Padania and federal. However, there is no mention of any intention for regional independence in the near future. Salvini only mentions regional autonomy on a few occasions, not just for the Northern regions but for all Italian regions, using northern regions as a reference point of efficiency. It is worth noting that Salvini's federalist discourse in government focuses more on the idea of regional autonomy as a priority for the government without necessarily providing concrete achievements or goals. At the same time, his federalist discourse in opposition uses language that recalls the idea of regional independence without advocating for it directly.

Conclusion

This chapter explored Salvini's social media rhetoric and its consistency over time. It reveals that political and social events influence his rhetoric, but the overall salience remains unaffected. Salvini's social media rhetoric emphasizes nativism, authoritarianism, populism, and Euroskepticism as the most salient ideological discourses, whether in government or opposition. However, religion and federalism are not prominent ideologies in Salvini's social media discourse. Regarding coherence in delivering these ideologies, the results show that all ideological discourses, except for populism, are coherent whether Salvini is in government or opposition. Interestingly, Salvini's social media rhetoric appears to be more moderate when focusing on his populist discourse, being less emotional while in government than in opposition.

Furthermore, only nativism, Euroskepticism, populism, and federalism have narratives strictly linked to their domains, while

---

[58]   The original text: Ho voglia di condividere la mia gioia con voi! Lavoro, meno tasse, immigrazione, pace fiscale, pensioni, autonomia, sicurezza: dalle parole ai fatti! ● LIVE > https://t.co/Th3j3Sppxf https://t.co/97rdqRYn2u.

authoritarianism and religion are used as proxies to discuss narratives linked to nativism. This analysis suggests that Salvini's social media rhetoric is highly influenced by nativism, which he uses to construct his social media rhetoric. Moreover, we believe that these findings have one fundamental implication.

Such influence of the nativist discourse has the potential to influence the Italian (and European) party politics significantly. In fact, as Wodak (2021:6) describes it, the unsayable is suddenly becoming sayable, leading to a "shameless normalization" of radical right discourses (see also Krzyżanowski, 2020). Scholars have already confirmed that social media platforms (including Twitter) play a crucial role in such a normalization process (see, e.g., Smith and Higgins, 2020; Popescu and Vesalon, 2022). Moreover, the pivotal role of Matteo Salvini within Italian politics further normalizes populist radical right-wing discourses. First, there is no moderate right-wing political alternative in Italian party politics at present. Second, Salvini has held important institutional roles, such as deputy prime minister, minister of the interior in the first Conte government, and minister of infrastructure and sustainable mobility in Meloni's government. Such roles provide a platform for radical right-wing politicians to promote their ideas and beliefs, influencing public discourse and opinion.

In conclusion, the influence of nativist discourse in Italian (and European) party politics is a significant issue that requires attention. The normalization of radical right-wing ideologies, enabled by social media like Twitter and powerful politicians like Salvini, has the potential to influence public opinion and change the political landscape in Italy and Europe.

References

Albertazzi, D., and McDonnell, D. (2010). The Lega Nord back in government. *West European Politics*, 33(6), 1318-1340.

Barrie, C., and Ho, J. C. T. (2021). academictwitteR: an R package to access the Twitter Academic Research Product Track v2 API endpoint. *Journal of Open Source Software*, 6(62), 3272.

Benoit, K., Watanabe, K., Wang, H., Nulty, P., Obeng, A., Müller, S., and Matsuo, A. (2018). quanteda: An R package for the quantitative analysis of textual data. *Journal of Open Source Software*, 3(30), 774.

Bernhard, L. (2020). Revisiting the inclusion-moderation thesis on radical right populism: Does party leadership matter? *Politics and Governance*, 8(1), 206-216.

Berti, C., and Loner, E. (2021). Character assassination as a right-wing populist communication tactic on social media: The case of Matteo Salvini in Italy. *New Media & Society*, 14614448211039222.

Biorcio, R. (1991). La Lega come attore politico: dal federalismo al populismo regionalista. In R. Mannheimer (Ed.), *La Lega Lombarda* (pp. 34-82). Feltrinelli: Milano.

Biorcio, R. (1997). La padania promessa, la storia, le idee e la logica d'azione della Lega Nord. Milano: Il Saggiatore.

Borbáth, E., and Gessler, T. (2023). How do populist radical right parties differentiate their appeal? Evidence from the Media Strategy of the Hungarian Jobbik Party. *Government and Opposition, 58(1)*, 84-105.

Bull, A. C., and Gilbert, M. (2001). *The Lega Nord and the northern question in Italian politics*. Houndmills & New York: Palgrave.

Caiani, M., and Conti, N. (2014). In the name of the people: The Euroskepticism of the Italian radical right. *Perspectives on European Politics and Society*, 15(2), 183-197.

De Winter, L. (2003). Conclusion: A comparative analysis of the electoral, office and policy success of ethnoregionalist parties. In L. De Winter (Ed.) Regionalist Parties in Western Europe (pp. 222-265). London: Routledge.

Diamanti, I. (1995). L'improbabile ma rischiosa secessione. *Il Mulino*. Bologna: Il Mulino, 44(5), 811-820.

Diamanti, I., and Donaldson, J. (1997). The Lega Nord: From Federalism to Secession. *Italian Politics*, 12, 65-81.

Donà, A. (2020). The populist Italian Lega from ethno-regionalism to radical right-wing nationalism: Backsliding gender-equality policies with a little help from the anti-gender movement. *European Journal of Politics and Gender*, 3(1), 161–163.

Feinerer I., and Hornik, K. (2020). tm: Text Mining Package. *R package version 0.7-8*.

Giordano, B. (2000). Italian regionalism or 'Padanian' nationalism — the political project of the Lega Nord in Italian politics. *Political Geography*, 19(4), 445-471.

Gold, T. W. (2003). *The Lega Nord and contemporary politics in Italy*. London: Macmillan.

Gómez-Reino Cachafeiro, M. (2004). La Lega Nord: mobilisation et revendication du "nationalisme padan". *Pôle Sud, 20*(1), 133-146.

Ivaldi, G., Lanzone, M. E., and Woods, D. (2017). Varieties of Populism across a Left-Right Spectrum: The Case of the Front National, the Northern League, Podemos and Five Star Movement. *Swiss Political Science Review, 23*(4), 354-376.

Kitschelt, H., and McGann, A. J. (1997). *The radical right in Western Europe: A comparative analysis.* Ann Arbor: University of Michigan Press.

Krzyżanowski, M. (2020). Discursive shifts and the normalisation of racism: Imaginaries of immigration, moral panics and the discourse of contemporary right-wing populism. *Social Semiotics, 30*(4), 503-527.

Mannheimer, R. (1991). Chi vota Lega e perché. In R. Mannheimer (Ed.) *La Lega Lombarda,* (pp. 122-158). Milano: Feltrinelli.

Mudde, C. (2004). The populist zeitgeist. *Government and opposition, 39*(4), 541-563.

Natale, P. (2018), I due elettorati del nuovo governo, *Comunicazione politica, Quadrimestrale dell'Associazione Italiana di Comunicazione Politica,* 2, 273-276.

Popescu, L., and Vesalon, L. (2022). "They all are the red plague": anti-communism and the Romanian radical right populists. *East European Politics,* 1-20.

Quaglia, L. (2008). Euroskepticism in Italy. In Szczerbiak, A., and Taggart, P. A. (Eds). *Opposing Europe? Volume 2, Comparative and Theoretical Perspectives: The Comparative Party Politics of Euroskepticism* (pp. 58-74). Oxford: Oxford University Press.

Reveilhac, M., and Morselli, D. (2022). Dictionary-based and machine learning classification approaches: a comparison for tonality and frame detection on Twitter data. *Political Research Exchange, 4*(1), 2029217.

Scopelliti, A. (2020), Populism in Power: the Italian Case, in Leidig, E. (Ed.). *Mainstreaming the Global Radical Right: CARR Yearbook 2019/2020.* Stuttgart: ibidem-Verlag.

Smith, A., and Higgins, M. (2020). Tough guys and little rocket men: @ RealDonaldTrump's Twitter feed and the normalisation of banal masculinity. *Social Semiotics, 30*(4), 547-562.

Stier, S., Bleier, A., Lietz, H., and Strohmaier, M. (2018). Election campaigning on social media: Politicians, audiences, and the mediation of political communication on Facebook and Twitter. *Political communication, 35*(1), 50-74.

Szczerbiak, A. and Taggart, P. A. (2008). *Opposing Europe? Volume 2, Comparative and Theoretical Perspectives: The Comparative Party Politics of Euroskepticism*. Oxford: Oxford University Press.

Wickham, H., François, R., Henry, L., and Müller, K. (2022). dplyr: A Grammar of Data Manipulation. *R package version 1.0-9*.

Wodak, R. (2021). *The politics of fear: the shameless normalization of far-right discourse*. London: SAGE.

Zaslove, A. (2011). *The re-invention of the European radical right: populism, regionalism, and the Italian Lega Nord*. McGill-Queen's Press-MQUP.

Chapter 4
The Foundation, Rise and Affirmation of Fratelli d'Italia (2012-2022)

A decade in the life of Fratelli d'Italia (2012-2022)

In her tell-all memoir titled *Io sono Giorgia. Le mie radici, le mie idee* (Meloni 2021, 183-185), Giorgia Meloni delves deeply into personal aspects of her political life. She reveals that between the latter part of 2018 and the early months of 2019, she seriously contemplated stepping down from her role as leader of the right-wing party Fratelli d'Italia (Brothers of Italy or FdI). This period marked half a decade since the founding of FdI, and it had only managed to muster an underwhelming 3-4 percent in terms of electoral results. In comparison, her counterpart Matteo Salvini successfully led his party, Lega (the League), to an impressive 35 percent during the same time. However, according to Meloni, the pivotal moment came during the European Parliament elections that took place in May 2019. In this crucial event, FdI defied expectations by obtaining a respectable 6.44 percent of the vote. Meloni believes this result not only granted FdI a much-needed boost but also helped the party break free from the 'voto utile' (useful vote) gray area—where a vote cast for a party that does not manage to cross the threshold is deemed useless (Ibid., 186-187). In that very same European Parliament election, Lega achieved a remarkable victory by securing 34.26 percent of the public's support (while FI garnered 8.78 percent). This impressive showing allowed Salvini to emerge as the clear successor to Silvio Berlusconi as the leading figure within Italy's right-wing political spectrum. As a result, Salvini came to occupy what authors Daniele Albertazzi and Duncan McDonnell have described as "the sun of the Italian rightwing galaxy", a position that Berlusconi had held for a considerable time (Albertazzi and McDonnell 2009; also Albertazzi et al. 2021).

The limited influence that FdI experienced up until at least the years 2020-2021 could potentially account for the relatively small amount of research and studies conducted on this party, particularly when compared to other Italian populist radical-right parties (PRRPs), such as Lega. This observation held at least until September 2022. In stark contrast, Lega has been the subject of numerous captivating works and authoritative research, which have focused on its current 'national' or 'sovereignist' guise simply known as Lega (Albertazzi et al. 2018; De Luca and Fruncillo 2019; Passarelli and Tuorto 2018b[59]), as well as its former incarnation, Lega Nord, prior to the transformation that took place under the leadership of Salvini (Albertazzi and McDonnell 2005, 2010; Bull and Gilbert 2001; Tarchi 2003). This extensive academic inquiry had not been the case for FdI before 2022. In fact, prior to that year, there were only a limited number of scholarly works available on FdI. Most of these studies primarily concentrated on the right-wing coalition (Albertazzi et al. 2021; Castelli Gattinara and Froio 2021), although there were a few exceptions that focused specifically on FdI (Bruno and Downes 2020; Bruno, Downes and Scopelliti 2021)[60]. However, more recently, there has been an increase in studies on the FdI, including comprehensive monographs and other forms of scholarly work that contribute to a better understanding of this political party, such as the works by political scientists Vassallo and Vignati (2022), Davide Vampa (2023) and historian David Broder (2023).

The chapter, organized into three extensive sections, which broadly outlined the first decade of the life of FdI, aims at giving a comprehensive and detailed account of how the party surged in late 2012 relatively unnoticed following the well-known clash between Silvio Berlusconi and Gianfranco Fini in 2010, and the subsequent *crisi dello spread* in 2011, to become currently not only Italy's leading political party and the driving force behind the right-wing

---

[59] In a very interesting way, Passarelli and Tuorto (2018b) have framed Salvini's Lega as an extreme-right party.
[60] One reason may be found in the relative late foundation of the party (late 2012); yet for the *Movimento 5 Stelle* (Five Star Movement or M5S), founded in late 2009 by Beppe Grillo and Gianroberto Caseleggio, scholars and analysts have devoted much more attention, producing an important number of authoritative studies and researches (Bickerton & Accetti 2018; Mosca 2014; Tronconi 2015; Mosca & Tronconi 2019; Passarelli & Tuorto 2018; Pirro 2018; Vampa 2015, only to mention some).

coalition but potentially the pioneer of the convergence at the EU level between the 'souverainist' right-wing populists and the conservatives.

a) The Prelude: April 2010–December 2012
This section provides an in-depth understanding of the context and a detailed account of events that ultimately led Giorgia Meloni and some of her colleagues not to follow Gianfranco Fini in his new political project in 2010, under Futuro e Libertà per l'Italia (FLI). It delves into why they chose to split from Silvio Berlusconi's PDL and subsequently form a new party. It discusses the underlying factors including the backdrop of the eurozone crisis with regards to the Italian spread as well as the technocratic government led by Mario Monti.

b) Birth and 'build-up': December 2012–May 2019
This section closely examines a period that could be characterized as one involving considerable patience and anticipation. Despite experiencing a series of unsatisfactory election results for FdI during this time, two national congresses—Fiuggi in 2014 and Trieste in 2017—were conducted. The turning point came with the European Parliament elections held in May 2019. This broader time frame encompasses two Italian general elections that took place in 2013 and 2018.

c) Rise and Affirmation: May 2019 – September 2022
This section explores the period of FdI's ascent, which began with the European Parliament election in May 2019. It covers a range of important events, including the party's position against the yellow-green coalition of M5S and Lega in Conte Cabinet I, its reaction to the COVID-19 pandemic during the Draghi cabinet era, the 'lone' opposition to Draghi's executive, and its stance on the Russia-Ukraine war. Additionally, it dissects the initial dynamics within the broader right-wing coalition, specifically in relation to Lega and their challenge for leadership.

The prelude: the Berlusconi-Fini 'clash' and the crisis of the spread (April 2010–December 2012)

As previously mentioned, FdI was founded on December 21, 2012, by Giorgia Meloni, Ignazio La Russa and Guido Crosetto[61]. Meloni and La Russa had backgrounds in the dissolved political parties Alleanza Nazionale (National Alliance, AN[62]) and Movimento Sociale Italiano (Italian Social Movement, MSI. On the MSI see Ignazi, 1994, 171-190). The new political formation emerged during a tumultuous period in Italian and European history. In fact, between late 2011 and 2012, Italy found itself squarely in the midst of the *crisi dello spread*, which was the nation's 'share' of the broader European sovereign debt crisis. The multi-year debt crisis unfolded within the EU and was especially challenging for countries labeled as PIGS (Portugal, Italy, Greece, and Spain) or PIIGS (with the addition of Ireland)[63]. In Italy, this period culminated in November 2021 with Silvio Berlusconi's sudden resignation as prime minister amidst growing chaos[64]. Following Berlusconi's departure from office,

---

[61] Source: Fratelli d'Italia website (https://www.fratelli-italia.it/team-wsidebar/).
[62] Gianfranco Fini was the leader of Alleanza Nazionale from its very foundation in 1995 at the convention of Fiuggi through 2008, when he was elected President of Italy's Chamber of Deputies. For the complex relationship with Giorgia Meloni, see Meloni (2021).
[63] The ongoing financial instability followed closely on the heels of the global financial crisis that spanned 2007-2008. The global financial crisis had its origins in the United States when the subprime mortgage bubble burst and ultimately led to the collapse of Lehman Brothers, one of the largest investment banks worldwide at that time (Tooze, 2018).
[64] Italian citizens quickly became familiar with the risk of financial default, the possible reaction of financial markets, the "spread" (the differential between interest rates on local public debts and Germany's) or the action of the Troika (EU Commission, IMF and European Central Bank, with months characterized first by fear and then by frustration, and the relative instrumentalization of these. On the role of fear and its instrumentalization during the *crisi dello spread*, Bruno wrote for *Social Europe*: "Fears produced by technocratic elites in Europe are based on complex and specific arguments, posed in technical and bureaucratic language, with masterly timing: using specific moments of political instability or paralysis that result in uncertainty to justify the necessity of implementing the political agenda they support. Mentioning the possible reaction of financial markets, the 'spread' (the differential between interest rates on local public debts and Germany's) or the action of the Troika (EC, IMF and ECB), has become increasingly common, in what takes on the traits of a self-fulfilling

Mario Monti was appointed to form a new cabinet by President of the Republic Giorgio Napolitano[65]. Intriguingly, this occurred without an official government crisis declaration or a call for regular elections to establish a new governing body[66]. It is evident that Meloni and her colleagues' crucial decision to create FdI was influenced by the context of the expansive European sovereign debt crisis (2009–2013). However, it is possible to pinpoint at least three driving factors that ultimately pushed Meloni to make the difficult decision to split from Berlusconi's PDL and establish a new political party with La Russa and Crosetto (Meloni, 161–177):

> "Clearly, the origin of Fratelli d'Italia is deeply rooted in the various crises occurring between 2007 and 2012, which shaped its formation and the motivations of its founders. The decision to break away from traditional political parties and establish a new political entity was influenced by a combination of global, European, and domestic factors that were interwoven at that time. Expanding upon these points can offer further insights into both the historical context surrounding FdI's formation and the political landscape that emerged as a result".

---

prophecy. More and more frequently, we record statements from high-level EU bureaucrats or politicians such as 'the risk of default will eventually lead to...', etc. In particular, before and after referendums or elections, continual references are made to possible sovereign debt defaults or the risk deriving from re-defining the Maastricht criteria (in Italy, from 2011 until recently) or the economic price to be paid for leaving the EU (in the United Kingdom, in the wake of Brexit in 2016), resulting in limiting de facto the space for political debate". (Bruno 2018, also Bruno 2020).

[65] Italy is a fully-fledged parliamentary republic. Yet, as it will be seen also in other occasions, the FdI's request of election and aversion for government cabinets established upon nomination of the President of the Republic in times of crisis is frequent, represents almost a *topos*.

[66] Which is however perfectly fine according to Italy's constitution and status as parliamentary democracy.

Figure 4.1 The current logo of Fratelli d'Italia (left) and The Movimento Sociale Italiano (The Italian Social Movement or MSI) with the Tricolor Flame

(i) The primary reason that Giorgia Meloni finds perplexing is the seemingly inexplicable support exhibited by Silvio Berlusconi's People of Freedom party (PDL) toward Mario Monti's technocratic administration. While there was an initial endorsement from various factions due to the precarious and dramatic circumstances surrounding the political landscape at that time, Meloni has remained consistent in her belief that Monti's technocratic government was not organic but rather an orchestrated effort imposed from above. According to Meloni's perspective, this scheme involved a multitude of key players and influential entities working behind the scenes. These included high-ranking bureaucrats situated within the EU's power base in Brussels, a collaboration between prominent French and German political figures known as the Franco-German alliance, and even the tacit approval and complicity of Italy's president during that era, Giorgio Napolitano. As a result, Meloni has expressed concern that the entire political episode could be construed as a calculated conspiracy to subvert democratic norms within Italy. Her apprehensions are directly voiced in her own words, as she articulates her standpoint on this matter in her book published in 2021 (Meloni 2021, 168). The collaboration might have conceivably allowed for covert manipulation of Italy's government by promoting Monti's technocratic leadership despite its questionable legitimacy and potential ulterior motives:

> "I told Berlusconi, clearly, that the People of Freedom should absolutely not have given support to the Monti government. It was intolerable to hand Italy over to the emissaries of those European consortiums that had maneuvered against our democracy; it was like saying that our adversaries were right, and they weren't. [[...]] Very few others followed my reasoning that evening. And at a certain point I understood: they had given up, Berlusconi first. Perhaps, thinking back, the first spark of the flame that led me to found Fratelli d'Italia a year later was that evening [Author's note: 12 November 2011], looking at the faces of a political class that no longer had the strength to fight. For me it was not like that" (Translation by the authors).[67]

(ii) The secondary rationale behind this conflict, which can be considered a traditional *casus belli*, stemmed from Silvio Berlusconi's unexpected move in early December 2012. Berlusconi abruptly decided to call off the PDL primaries, wherein Meloni was actively involved in an electoral race against Angelino Alfano. At that moment, Alfano appeared to be Berlusconi's chosen successor or protégé. This narrative has been documented and corroborated by Meloni herself in her 2021 publication (pages 171–172), as well as the research conducted by Vassallo and Vignati in their 2023 work.

(iii) The third motivation is by far the most relevant. It is connected to both (a) ideological aspects that have their foundation in the so-called post-fascist tradition of FdI within MSI and AN and (b) the conflict between Gianfranco Fini and Silvio Berlusconi that culminated in April 2010. Throughout this time, Meloni did not particularly agree with Fini's decision in March 2008 to merge AN with Berlusconi's PDL. Meloni once stated, "For Berlusconi, I have

---

[67] Original text in Italian. "Dissi a Berlusconi, con chiarezza, che il Popolo della Libertà non avrebbe dovuto assolutamente dare l'appoggio al governo Monti. Era intollerabile consegnare l'Italia agli emissari di quelle consorterie europee che avevano manovrato contro la nostra democrazia; era come dire che avevano ragione i nostri avversari, e non l'avevano. [[...]] Pochissimi altri mi seguirono nel ragionamento, quella sera. E a un certo punto capii: si erano arresi, Berlusconi in testa. Forse, ripensandoci, la prima scintilla di quella fiamma che mi ha portato di lì ad un anno a fondare Fratelli d'Italia è scoccata quella sera [nda 12 November 2011], guardando i volti di una classe politica che non aveva più la forza di combattere. Per me non era così." (Meloni, 168).

always been an anthropological difference that is difficult to accept wholly, both as an individual and as a representative of another political culture. We remained loyal allies but often diverged on our approach to politics" (Meloni, 87)[68]. AN was a relatively new political party formed after the 'Fiuggi turn' in 1995. This event marked the transformation of the MSI, established in 1946 following the end of World War II, into AN under Gianfranco Fini's guidance. Fiuggi is a small town with a population of around 10,000 located in the province of Frosinone, about seventy kilometers from Rome. It served as the venue for both the final MSI national congress and the constituent congress of the newly formed AN on January 27, 1995. In Fiuggi, the secretary of the emerging party declared an official separation from fascism and those ambiguities that had defined MSI in its earlier days. This shift signaled a move toward embracing a fully republican and democratic right-wing ideology and marked the official beginning of the post-fascism era. Meloni found it even more challenging to accept Fini's decision to part ways with Berlusconi and establish a new party called Futuro e Libertà per l'Italia (Ibid. 105–106). Reflecting on this, she said,

> "I still cannot comprehend Fini's choices. I struggle to fathom how the man who had dedicated his entire life to fostering the growth of Italy's right wing and, owing to his skill and intuition, steered it from the fringes of the constitutional arch into a potent governing force could, within months, do everything in his power to dismantle that legacy" (Ibid.)[69].

As history unfolded, Fini's newly formed party took part in a vote of no confidence against the Berlusconi IV government on December 2, 2010; however, their attempt was unsuccessful. Fast forward

---

[68] Original text in Italian. "Io, per Berlusconi, sono sempre stata una diversità antropologica difficile da accettare completamente, sia come persona, sia come esponente di una cultura politica altra. Alleati leali, ma spesso distanti nel modo di concepire la politica". The English translation is by the authors.

[69] Original text in Italian. "Ancora oggi non riesco a spiegarmi le scelti di Gianfranco Fini. Non mi capacito di come l'uomo che aveva dedicato una vita a far crescere la destra in Italia, e che grazie alla sua abilità e alle sue intuizioni l'aveva tirata fuori dai margini dell'arco costituzionale per farne una forza di governo, in pochi mesi abbia fatto tutto ciò che poteva per distruggere quel patrimonio". The English translation is by the authors.

a decade to 2022[70], Ignazio La Russa, another major political figure during that period, was interviewed by Italian newspaper *Repubblica* (April 22, 2020):

> "That day was the epilogue of a clash that had been going on for some time. The personal incompatibility between Silvio and Gianfranco weighed more than the political fact: Fini did not accept Berlusconi's landlord ways, and the latter resented the former's leading role. [[...]] For me it was a lacerating suffering: I did everything to avoid this clash, before and after. I would have supported Fini if he had challenged Berlusconi from the right, but instead he attacked him from the center, which was not our political space. I also proposed to him to resign as coordinator of the PDL in order to found a right-wing current within the party, but evidently Fini, to whom I also acknowledge great merits, already had something else on his mind".

Returning to the topic of Giorgia Meloni, it is important to consider the significant differences that have developed over time between her and both Silvio Berlusconi and Gianfranco Fini. These variances, as well as the interplay between these two essential figures within the right-wing coalition, were instrumental in the formation of Brothers of Italy (FdI). Even though Meloni is politically indebted to both Berlusconi and Fini, their respective political agendas, particularly Fini's direction, have been met with skepticism by Meloni and other members of the National Alliance-Movement Social Italian (AN-MSI) grouping. In essence, Fini's decision to initially incorporate AN into Berlusconi's dominant PDL project, followed by his subsequent choice to distance himself from Berlusconi with a more moderate right-wing endeavor, likely left both Meloni and much of the former AN-MSI leadership perplexed. This discontentment was eloquently articulated by Vassallo and Vignati (2023). While there are clear distinctions in political culture and party leadership ideologies that separate Meloni from Berlusconi, it is undeniable that both Meloni and her colleagues perceived Fini's latest political initiative as an unfavorable departure toward a 'modern right' movement which was incompatible with those who identify within the MSI's historical-cultural tradition. As Meloni (2021) suggests, this development marked a considerable shift away from their core

---

[70] Later, in the years of the technocratic government led by Mario Monti (end of 2011-2012), FLI supported the executive.

beliefs. Expanding upon this analysis, it becomes apparent that while the 1994-1995 transition from MSI to AN was begrudgingly accepted for numerous reasons, the 2008 amalgamation between AN and FI proved much more contentious. Confusion propagated by Fini's unexpected U-turn was seen as wholly unnecessary by many and ultimately led him to part ways with Berlusconi in 2010. Consequently, this conflict prompted the inception of a new political project, 'Future and Freedom for Italy' (FLI), which was relatively short-lived, spanning from 2011 to 2013. In retrospective contemplation, it is evident that the circumstances that culminated in the establishment of FdI in December 2012 could be interpreted as a comprehensive return to its original identity. This identity appeared to have been forsaken during the alliance with Berlusconi's PDL party and because of Fini's seemingly disoriented and unmoored leadership style. In summation, although some aspects may have initially appeared unexpected, tracing the steps that led to the creation of FdI clarifies this political evolution as deeply rooted in reestablishing an innate sense of self for its constituents[71].

---

[71] In examining the various elements and driving forces behind Fini's rise to the leadership position within AN, it is important to acknowledge the considerable distinctions that exist between him and a significant portion of MSI's political leadership. These differences extend even to Giorgio Almirante, an influential figure in his own right, who nonetheless openly endorsed Fini's leadership. The journey of Fini to the helm of AN is characterized by a complex interplay of motivations, political maneuvering, and divergent ideologies that merit a thorough exploration. For those interested in delving deeper into this fascinating narrative and better understanding the intricate details surrounding Fini's ascent to prominence within the party, Vassallo and Vignati's comprehensive analysis from their 2023 work serves as an invaluable resource. It should be emphasized that, while it might seem straightforward on the surface, unraveling the myriad nuances and implications of these intriguing dynamics often necessitates an in-depth examination from multiple angles. By doing so, one can gain a more complete appreciation for the historical context, political landscape, and individual forces at play that contributed to Fini becoming a central figure within AN. As such, consulting sources like Vassallo and Vignati's work is strongly recommended for anyone eager to delve into this topic extensively and gain insights that can pave the way for a richer understanding of not only Fini's journey but also broader patterns within Italian politics.

Figure 4.2 Evolution of the logo of Fratelli d'Italia. On the left the logo of the party Alleanza Nazionale.

1993 lo storico simbolo di Alleanza Nazionale   2012 Il primo simbolo del partito della Meloni   2014 Il vecchio simbolo con l'effetto "matrioska"   2017 Il nuovo simbolo di Fratelli d'Italia

Birth and 'build-up' of Fratelli d'Italia (December 2012–May 2019)

Just a few months after the inception of the FdI, they were faced with their inaugural electoral challenge during the general Italian election in February 2013. Unfortunately, the results were disappointing for the young party, receiving a meager 1.96% of the votes, which translated roughly to 667,000 preferences for their candidates. Therefore, they were able to secure only nine seats in the Italian parliament. During its initial stages, the leadership of Ignazio La Russa saw FdI through this testing time as they sought to establish themselves in Italy's political landscape. However, La Russa's tenure was short-lived and concluded in February 2014. This marked a turning point for the party as it transitioned to new leadership and explored different directions for its future. FdI conducted its first-ever national convention in March 2014, set against the picturesque backdrop of Fiuggi—a town known not only for its beauty but also for its historical significance and eloquence, befitting such an important event. It was during this gathering that Giorgia Meloni emerged as a strong and unifying figure within the party. Affirming her position as a leader who could bring about change and growth, she secured unanimous support from her peers to become FdI's secretary. This pivotal moment in FdI's history saw Meloni take on the mantle of leadership and steer the party toward new horizons. Despite initially struggling in their first electoral test, FdI regrouped under Meloni's guidance and continued with renewed vigor to find their place within Italian politics. With an unwavering commitment to their core values and a clear vision for the future, FdI and its members have embraced continuous learning and improvement while adapting to changing national dynamics.[72] In the following month, the party leadership opted to leave the (EPP) in strong disagreement with the common currency, the Euro, and Germany's handling of the so-called Eurozone sovereign debt crisis[73].

During the second ballot box test, specifically the European Parliament election that took place in Italy in May of 2014, FdI once again experienced a disappointing outcome, managing to secure a mere 3.66% of the overall votes. This percentage fell short of the minimum threshold required (4%) for a party's elected representatives to take their place as Members of European Parliament (MEPs) and be seated in Strasbourg. In stark contrast, the Democratic Party (PD), under the leadership of Matteo Renzi—a young and promising political figure at the time—achieved a remarkable victory by garnering a staggering 40.8% of the total votes cast. This impressive result firmly established PD as a dominant force during that particular election cycle.[74] In the meantime, the Monti executive had

---

[72] It is not a coincidence that a convention was also held in Fiuggi that saw the birth of AN under the leadership of Gianfranco Fini in 1995. Source:- https://www.fratelli-italia.it/2014/03/06/fdi-an-sabato-e-domenica-a-fiuggi-il-primo-congresso-nazionale/.

[73] On the leadership role of Germany in Europe in the period 2008-2018, see at least Bruno & Finzi (2018).

[74] In recent times, there has been a growing importance to discuss and analyze the initial years of the FdI party. A pertinent question that has emerged is whether the party's leadership had always established a clear vision for the type of political party they intended to form, or did their ideology evolve over time? Scholars Vignati and Vassallo (2023) suggest that at its inception, FdI started out with a specific political stance, but later on shifted their focus towards a different direction. Analyzing manifestos and official declarations from various sources provides insight into the party's identity over time. Donà (2022, 784) asserts that up until the 2017 Trieste Congress, FdI exhibited a conservative right-wing identity. However, subsequent events indicate that the party gravitated towards adopting a populist radical-right stance. During the 2014 Fiuggi Congress, it was observed that no emphasis was placed on nativism, nationalism, or authoritarianism in their manifesto. Furthermore, there were no blatant anti-immigration or xenophobic undertones present either. Consequently, it can be deduced that at that juncture, FdI maintained an ideological profile

succeeded one led by the member of the PD, Enrico Letta, in a sort of government of broad agreements ('governo di larghe intese', in Italian) also supported by Berlusconi's PDL, until February 22, 2013, when the PD itself retired its support, with the just mentioned Renzi, freshly elected as new PD secretary, forming the new cabinet and becoming at 39 the youngest Italian Prime Minister ever. FdI, in those years, remained in opposition, differently from Berlusconi's PDL (which, in the meantime, had moved back to the old party name of *FI*)[75].

In the 2016 and 2017 Italian local elections, FdI collected some interesting but isolated results at the ballot box, either running alone or in lists with the center-right coalition (FdI, Lega and FI). For instance, in 2016, the victory for the mayor of the town of Isernia (Giacomo D'Apollonio) in the region of Molise and the positive performances in Rome (12.28%), Novara, Grosseto, Latina, and Pordenone (in all the cities more than 5%, and in the latter, the party also gained the seat of the mayor)[76].

In 2017, the seat of the mayor of the city of L'Aquila (Pierluigi Biondi) was gained with 35.84%, with good performances (more than 5%) obtained by FdI mayor candidates in the cities of La Spezia, Asti, Gorizia, Genova, Piacenza, Rieti and Lecce, to name a

---

closely resembling a conservative right-wing party. However, significant changes in FdI's core beliefs began to surface shortly after. These transformations in their ideology became apparent when Giorgia Meloni — the party leader — delivered her concluding address at the first party congress 'In the name of the sovereign people.' This event took place on March 9, 2014 in Fiuggi and occurred just a few months prior to the European Parliament (E.P.) elections. During Meloni's speech at this occasion, elements consistent with populist radical-right parties (R.R.P.) became evident in FdI's ideological framework. The party started to display heightened nationalism and authoritarian inclinations, accompanied by clear signs of Euro-skepticism. As a result, FdI's political profile underwent a noticeable shift, distancing itself from its previous conservative right-wing stance and moving towards the populist radical-right spectrum.

[75] It is important to note that on occasion in the Letta executive (2013–2014) and during the early phases of the Renzi cabinet (2014–early 2015) Berlusconi had granted its support to those executives, first with *Il Popolo della Libertà* and later with the revival of *Forza Italia* (September 2013), with the so called 'patto del Nazareno' (The Nazareno pact).

[76] https://www.interno.gov.it/it/speciali/elezioni-amministrative-5-giugno-2016

few[77]. During this period, nationally, the FdI actively campaigned against the 2016 Italian constitutional referendum, also referred to as the 'Riforma costituzionale Renzi-Boschi'. This significant amendment to the Italian Constitution was ardently championed by then-Prime Minister Matteo Renzi and his cabinet. The key basis of the referendum involved consulting Italian voters on a constitutional law aimed at altering the makeup and jurisdiction of the parliament. The proposed changes also sought to redefine the distribution of power between the state, regional authorities, and administrative bodies. As 2016 ended, this monumental referendum ultimately failed. The implications of this outcome reverberated across Italy's political landscape, leading to a crisis within Renzi's cabinet and prompting him to resign from his position as prime minister. In the aftermath, a new executive government was formed under Paolo Gentiloni, who had previously assumed the role of minister of foreign affairs during Renzi's tenure. The formation of this new government marked a turning point within Italian politics. Following these events in 2017, an influx of deputies from (FI) decided to leave Silvio Berlusconi's party and join forces with FdI. Among these prominent figures were Stefano Bertacco, Bartolomeo Amidei, and Daniela Santanchè. Their decision to transition from FI to Fratelli d'Italia signified a notable shift in political alliances as they sought to support FdI's stance concerning governance structure reform within Italy. In essence, this longer rendition maintains the original content and structure while elaborating on certain aspects for a more comprehensive explanation of the events surrounding the FdI's campaign against the 2016 Italian constitutional referendum.

The Trieste congress (2017) and the 2018 Italian general election

In December 2017, exactly five years after its foundation, FdI closed the year celebrating its second national congress, held in Trieste on December 2-3 [78]. According to Donà (2022, 785-786), who analyzes

---

[77] https://www.interno.gov.it/it/speciali/elezioni-amministrative-11-giugno-2017
[78] See the document available at: https://www.fratelli-italia.it/wp-content/uploads/2017/09/INDICAZIONI-ORGANIZZATIVE-CONGRESSO.pdf

the programmatic document *Le Tesi di Trieste per il movimento dei patrioti* (2017):

> "... The second party convention held in Trieste in 2017 formalized the radical right shift of FdI. On this occasion, the articulated document 'Thesis of Trieste for the movement of the Patriots' was approved and it represented the ideological platform upon which were later elaborated the 2018 national and 2019 E.P. electoral programmes – and again for the upcoming snap elections."

The 2017 FdI's political document emphasizes the centrality of the national identity, conceived as the expression of a single and homogeneous community sharing a common history, cultural heritage and traditional values. FdI claims the "rediscovery of the identity, the return to the traditional values and the renewal of the belonging to a single national community" (FdI 2017, 4) in contrast to damage by the progressive culture. Hence, the role of FdI as a protector of national interests and national identity was proclaimed. In the first section, titled "A philosophy of the identity" (FdI 2017, 1), patriotism and national identity are the key concepts upon which is built the ideological populist framework which opposes the 'patriots' against untrue patriots and threatening others and especially against the European project.[79]

In 2018, the Italian general election took place, and it was marked by several significant changes that set it apart from previous elections. The 2018 election was conducted under the new electoral system called Rosatellum. This mixed proportional system allocated 37% of the seats (232 in the House of Deputies and 116 in the Senate) through a majoritarian method while distributing 61% of the seats (386 and 193, respectively) proportionally among

---

[79] Donà's thesis of a gradual veering by FdI from (a) rightwing conservative party position toward (b) a populist radical right-wing party (PRRP), featuring nativist and authoritarian core elements, would have started in 2014 to be then fully implemented in 2017, caused by the instability affecting the Italian party system and the recurring EU crises during the last decade, has undoubtedly many convincing points. One point that could be raised, however, concerns the doubts and distrust of Meloni and La Russa, among others, toward the positions of Gianfranco Fini and his political project (FLI), which, according to Dona (2022, 781) would have been "building a mainstream conservative right-wing party", if FdI was supposed to go towards the same direction.

120   THE RISE OF THE RADICAL RIGHT IN ITALY

coalitions and individual lists that surpassed the mandatory national bar thresholds. This election marked a notable moment in Italy's political history as Silvio Berlusconi, ineligible to run for office due to the Severino law, still maintained his leadership position within FI. Despite not being able to run himself, Berlusconi forged a coalition with Lega and FdI, along with several other smaller center-right organizations. The fact that he could exercise such influence without being on the ballot was an extraordinary development. The election results presented an interesting picture. The center-right coalition emerged as the overall winner, with approximately 37% of the vote.

Meanwhile, the single most-voted list belonged to the M5S, capturing more than 32% of the popular vote. Following behind them were the PD and its allies, with roughly 23% of votes cast. It is important to note that there was not a clear victor in this election; neither side could claim a decisive victory or mandate. With a voter turnout of 72.94%, one must examine further the regional distribution of party support. M5S received overwhelming support in Central and Southern Italy, but their momentum did not carry them to win in Northern regions.

On the other hand, Lega dominated in Northern Italy but did not see comparable levels of success further south. Delving deeper into coalition support patterns shows an even more divided picture across Italy. The center-north region was primarily supportive of the right-wing coalition, while the South massively voted for M5S. This sharp divide created a political deadlock, with neither side having a commanding lead or clear path to consolidating power[80].

As mentioned, FdI also, on that occasion, joined forces with usual coalition partners, FI and the Lega[81], obtaining (also in this case) a rather modest and disappointing electoral result (Meloni,

---

[80]   In summary, the 2018 Italian general election was marked by significant changes, such as the introduction of the Rosatellum electoral system and Silvio Berlusconi's continued influence in politics despite his ineligibility to run. The election results demonstrated a divided Italy in terms of both party and coalition support, with no clear winner emerging from the contest. This division across regions further exacerbated the complexities of Italian politics and governance, hinting at potential challenges and stalemates in the future.

[81]   Plus minor parties, as *Noi con l'Italia-UDC*.

181), which allowed the party to elect 50 MPs (32 at the Chamber of Deputies and 18 at the Senate of the Republic). With 1,429,550 votes, FdI became the third party of the right-wing coalition, with about 4.3% of the overall votes, following Lega (17.35%) and FI (14%)[82], obtaining 32 seats at the Chamber of Deputies and 18 seats at the Senate.

Table 4.2: Electoral performances for main Italian parties at the 2018 Italy general election (and comparison with the 2013 general election)

	% 2018 general election*	% 2013 general election*	% difference 2013-2018
Fratelli d'Italia	4,35	1,96	+2,39
Lega	17,35	4,09	+ 13,26
Forza Italia	14	21,56	-7,56
PD	18,76	25,43	-6,67
M5S	32,68	25,56	+7,12

Note: The percentage of the Italian 2013 and 2018 general elections refers to the Chamber of Deputies

The Rise and affirmation of Fratelli d'Italia (May 2019 – September 2022)

Arguably, the months following the 2018 general election until the election for the European Parliament in May 2019 are the most complicated period for FdI. In fact, the lowest point could be seen with leader Matteo Salvini decision to bring Lega into a 'contratto di governo' (government contract) with the populist party M5S, giving birth to the first Conte cabinet, led by PM Giuseppe Conte, in what was defined as the yellow-green government, a *sui generis* populist executive (Alonzi 2020; Bruno and Downes 2018; Giannetti et al. 2020; Valbruzzi 2018)[83]. Salvini's move, a real political gamble,

---

[82] The percentages refer to the Chamber of Deputies.
[83] The 'spread', or the difference between local public debt interest rates and Germany's, began rapidly increasing in the summer of 2018: "Both Italian deputy prime ministers, Luigi Di Maio (of M5S) and Salvini (of Lega), accused the financial markets and rating agencies of being behind Mattarella's decision [to nominate a new technical cabinet]". Additionally, they made references to the EU's meddling in Italian politics and undermining of Italian sovereignty. This

produced quite possibly the most populist Italian government ever, with the leader having strategically obtained the post of minister of the interior by continually being the focus of media attention through his politics of 'blocking the ports' via ad hoc narratives to counter what was defined as invasions by migrants supported by NGOs while the M5S, which never really countered Salvini's strategy, focused mainly on the implementation of 'reddito di cittadinanza' (citizenship income).

For FdI and their leader Meloni (Meloni, 184–185), that was a turning point, a watershed moment when they decided not to support the yellow-green government. Bruno and Downes (2020) argued the importance of focusing on the FdI:

> After the 2018 general elections in Italy, the FdI was polling on average between 4% and 5%. Thus, the situation of the party was precarious and uncertain. In particular, the controversial decision by Matteo Salvini to form a government with the Italian 5-Star Movement (M5S) led by Luigi Di Maio could have potentially led to devastating consequences for both Meloni and her party, as the FdI and Berlusconi's *Forza Italia* were completely cut-off by the coalition government. However, Meloni demonstrated on that occasion her persistent personality. Perhaps judging that this coalition government would last only for a short period of time, Meloni resisted entering into agreement with it. Today [February 2020] the situation is completely different. The FdI has grown exponentially, with the latest polls in Italy giving FdI around 12% of the vote. Furthermore, in the last few months, the public image of Giorgia Meloni has also undergone a process of increased visibility and her *Fratelli d'Italia* Party has taken off in Italy.

In addition, Bruno and Downes (2020 noted the following about the increase in support for the FdI:

> This trend will most likely continue in the near future, as much of the electorate of *Forza Italia* has gradually been eroded and absorbed by the FdI. Two key factors can explain these trends, namely: (a) former Prime Minister Silvio Berlusconi's unwillingness to find a real political 'heir' for his party; and (b) the political ties and administrative structure of the two parties.

---

fostered M5S-Lega conspiracy theories, combined with the choice to propose a technocratic government led by Carlo Cottarelli (a former Director of the International Monetary Fund). 2018 (Bruno and Downes).

The 2019 European Parliament election as a turning point

Giorgia Meloni indicates in her autobiography that between early 2018 and the beginning of 2019, she was seriously considering resigning from the leadership of FdI, as was described at the beginning of the chapter (Meloni, 183–185). While her far-right colleague Matteo Salvini was rewarded for his plan of changing the party from Northern League to League, her party has not been able to gain more than 4% in five years (Albertazzi et al. 2018). The May 2019 elections for the European Parliament can be seen as a pivotal event for FdI. Salvini had run a campaign for the Italian Ministry of the Interior at the time, using the slogan: 'Stop burocrati[84], banchieri[85], buonisti[86], barconi[87]!' (Bruno 2022), in what can be considered

---

[84] The EU is a target for both the far-right and mainstream populist forces in Italy, particularly the 'Brussels bureaucrats'. The primary distinction is that, as opposed to the former, which alternates between harsh criticism of the European institutions, particularly the EC, and periods of gentler Euroskepticism, the latter maintains an attitude of stark and hard Euroskepticism. It is feasible to state that the element of euroskepticism has almost completely vanished in the case of Salvini's League, beginning with the Draghi government (February 2021). However, it will most likely reappear during the following political campaign. (Bruno 2022, 43–44).

[85] The use of the slang 'bankers' in a negative and allusive sense (bankers' servants or bankers' waiters) is well documented as far as the current Italian radical and extreme right is concerned. In particular, it is used widely by both (a) the mainstream radical right, the League and Brothers of Italy and (b) extreme-right neofascist movements and groups (for instance, Movimento Fascismo e Libertà). As far as the mainstream right is concerned, however, a fundamental difference can be seen starting with the election of Mario Draghi, former president of the European Central Bank, as Prime Minister from February 2021. Notably Salvini's League, part of Draghi's government, has begun to use the slang 'bankers' less and less for obvious reasons of political opportunism (Bruno 2022, 35-36).

[86] 'Buonisti' is an insult used by both the mainstream populist right and the far-right in Italy. The do-gooders would be the representatives of the left who defend, in a hypocritical manner, at least according to the radical right, illegal and unchecked immigration, a crime that threatens the order of the citizenry and the Italian military. Furthermore, in the narrative of the Italian radical right, buonisti are often intellectuals and elites who covertly advocate homogenization that leads to the loss of concepts such as identity, homeland, nation, and traditional family. (Bruno 2022, 42).

[87] "Barges" is the sadly well-known word used by the Italian media to describe the makeshift boats often used by immigrants, upon payment of large sums of money to criminal organizations to arrive clandestinely on Italian coasts, particularly from North Africa. However, some Italian radical-right politicians

as the peak of his popularity, with electoral polls assigning at the time something as above 35% of the preferences (a record that has not been reached by FdI even during the current days!). FdI at the European Parliament election of May 2019 obtained an unexpected 6,44% (Table 4.2), joining, among others, Poland's *PiS*, Spain's *Vox* and The Netherlands' *FvD*, in the ECR, a Euroskeptic, anti-federalist political group of the European Parliament accounting for 63 seats of the overall 705[88], which in September 2020 elected Meloni herself as its chairperson. This move may have important consequences considering the upcoming 2024 EP election[89].

Table 4.3 Electoral performances for main Italian parties at the European Parliament 2019 election (and comparison with EP 2014 election)

	% 2019 European Parliament election	% 2014 European Parliament election	% Difference
FdI	6,44	3,67	2,77
Lega	34,26	6,15	28,11
Forza Italia	8,78	16,81	-8,03
PD	22,74	40,81	-18,07
M5S	17,06	21,16	-4,1

After the first positive electoral performance in years, FdI did relatively well in local elections, obtaining overall strong results. In the 2018 local elections, FdI's performances was above 5% in terms of preferences in the cities of Terni, Viterbo, Teramo, Brindisi and

---

have made "barconi" slang to identify an allegedly uncontrolled invasion of Italy's borders by illegal immigrants. Matteo Salvini in particular became known for exploiting the issue strategically, with an intense campaign while he held the role of minister of the interior in the so-called "yellow-green coalition" (first Conte government June 2018–September 2019). In fact, for preventing some boats with people in poor condition on board, Salvini is currently under trial by the Italian judiciary (Bruno 2022, 37).

[88] The League obtained 28 seats for the Identity and Democracy Group, and Forza Italia 6 seats for the EPP Group.

[89] Italy's Giorgia Meloni elected president of European Conservatives and Reformists, *Politico*, 29 September 2020, https://www.politico.eu/article/italy-giorgia-meloni-ecr-president-european-parliament/.

Catania[90]. A few months later, confirming its further relevance in Central Italy's regions, FdI obtained its first regional presidency in Abruzzo, with Marco Marsilio (48% of the preference, with the center-left candidate at 31%), which was followed in late 2020 by Francesco Acquaroli as president of the Marche region (49% of the preferences, with the center-left candidate at 37.3%). Important results were also achieved with victories in the cities of Cagliari, Ascoli Piceno, Casale Monferrato, Ciampino, Scafati, Pagani, Piombino and Castel Volturno. In early September 2019, the first Conte cabinet was replaced by a second Conte cabinet, this time with the PD replacing Lega in the executive with the M5S. From a neutral stance, the FdI moved to a more authoritative opposition, producing important results in Calabria (10.58%) and Emilia-Romagna (8.59%).

COVID-19 and the FdI-Lega in neck and neck competition

Confirming the positive trend, the year 2019 ended with good electoral results in local elections, and 2020 opened similarly for FdI when the COVID-19 pandemic arrived suddenly, taking the world by surprise[91]. In fact, FdI has been performing extremely well since the first wave of the Covid-19 pandemic. The regional elections that took place together with the constitutional referendum to reduce the overall number of Italian MPs[92] showed two important elements: for the first time, a relative decline of the Lega and the strong decline of M5S, both benefiting in different ways FdI (Vassallo and Vignati, 2023). Bruno, Downes and Scopelliti (2020) provide an analysis of the strong decline of the M5S and the relative decline of the Lega. Concerning the M5S:

> "While the constitutional referendum result can be seen as a success for the M5S party, a broader look at the regional election results demonstrates a

---

[90] Source: la Repubblica, https://elezioni.repubblica.it/2018/elezioni-comunali.
[91] The impact of the COVID-19 pandemic on politics tout court is a controversial matter of ongoing debate worldwide. Rather clearly, the same caveat applies to the European political landscape and Italian politics (Mudde 2021; Mudde & Wondreys 2020; see also Bruno & Downes 2020b).
[92] The proposed referendum involved reducing the number of Italian MPs by 345, with 115 senators and 230 deputies (out of the 951) being cut in total.

bleaker picture for M5S in Italian politics. [...] Despite the fact that M5S has nearly always tended to underperform in regional elections, in comparison to general elections, it is clear that M5S is undergoing a broader process of electoral decline in their core electorate. For example, in Veneto, M5S saw a significant reduction in their vote share, from 10% in the 2015 regional election, to 3% in 2020. In Liguria, M5S declined even more, from 22% in 2015 to 8% in 2020. Similar electoral declines for M5S at the regional level can be seen in important regions, such as Tuscany, in Marche, alongside Campania and Puglia."

On the other hand, regarding the relative decline of the Lega, Bruno et al. commented (2020):

"The ambiguous policy stances of some Lega politicians on the constitutional referendum—with key members of the party such as Giancarlo Giorgetti, a former secretary of the council of the ministers and seen as a loyal supporter to Salvini, openly opposing it—has certainly not helped the party. In Veneto, Lega recorded the best performance amongst all the regions in Italy, with 77% of the vote. Nonetheless, this result exposes latent political contrasts within the party. The excellent performance of Luca Zaia (45%), a key member of the Lega, has further exposed the rivalry within the party between politicians (such as Zaia) that sustain the cleavages that founded the party (for example the autonomy of Veneto against the centralization of power in Rome) against those politicians (such as Salvini) that have nationalist ambitions and aim to control the 'center' rather than separate from it. Evidently, there are significant internal party disputes within Lega that continuously threaten the party's electoral fortunes. In Tuscany, and to a lesser extent in Apulia, the Lega performed relatively well, yet not enough to win. In the aftermath of the election Salvini, asked by journalists on the performance of his party and the alleged victory of the PD, rebuffed the notion, saying the center-right coalition overall governs in fifteen regions out of twenty in Italy and that Zingaretti's party did not have much to celebrate. Despite this electoral setback, Lega still command a large section of the electorate in Italy and remain an electoral force."

The Draghi executive and the re-election of Sergio Mattarella as Italy's head of State

Giorgia Meloni's party can be regarded as the true victor of the regional election in September 2020. Along with winning Tuscany and Emilia-Romagna, a historically 'red' stronghold, the FdI also performed well in all the regions where the elections were held, particularly in the region of Apulia (Bruno et al. 2020). While this is happening, a significant and somewhat unexpected event altered the dynamics of Italian politics. The stability of the second Conte cabinet, backed by M5S and PD, started to wane as early as December 2020, during yet another wave of COVID-19, in part due to criticism from former PM Matteo Renzi. Bruno (2021) reconstructs the complex situation of those months in the following way:

> "… When the government led by Prime Minister Giuseppe Conte was unable to find eleven lawmakers willing to join its ranks in the House of Representatives in order to keep his ruling majority, President Sergio Mattarella decided to offer the former president of the European Central Bank, Mario Draghi, the possibility to try to form a new *governo tecnico*. Italy's last technical government was led by Mario Monti between 2011 and 2012. A third Conte cabinet did not materialize because of the opposition by Matteo Renzi, the leader of Italia Viva, a party currently polling at 2%. All political parties in the Italian parliament supported Draghi's appointment except one: Giorgia Meloni's Fratelli d'Italia (Brothers of Italy). Even the Euroskeptic and anti-immigration populist-radical Lega (League) agreed to support Draghi, with its leader Matteo Salvini affirming, 'I rather prefer to play the game and manage 209 billions of euros than not', referring to the Italian share of the Next Generation EU plan agreed in July last year".[93]

While it is undeniable that the growth of FdI and the decline of the Lega and M5S (Bruno and Cozzolino 2021) began as early as 2019, the decision by Giorgia Meloni's party not to support Draghi's technocratic government has had fundamental and far-reaching consequences for Italian politics (Bruno, 2021). This can be read in relation to two complementary dynamics:

a) The FdI once more deployed the narrative of the party as being loyal to its principles and refusing to compromise. This card has previously been used quite a bit. As it was observed, the very act of 'being coherent with its own values and tradition' can be linked to the founding of FdI in late 2012. FI and FdI chose not to join Lega in the first Conte cabinet, more recently, in 2018, when Salvini strategically agreed to form a coalition government with Beppe Grillo's Movimento Cinque Stelle. Despite intense pressure to

---

[93] Next Generation EU, a €750-billion ($904-billlion) stimulus package designed to boost post-pandemic recovery, will be the largest ever financed by the European Union. Taken together with the EU's long-term budget, overall recovery funding stands at a total of €1.8 trillion, aimed at rebuilding, "a greener, more digital and more resilient Europe." (Bruno 2021).

support an executive which was once referred to as 'governo dei migliori' (government of the most competent) a few years later, this time with the Mario Draghi executive, FdI had preferred to remain in opposition. At the same time, the former president of the ECB was acclaimed as a savior, in almost messianic tones, in times when Italy faced the dual challenge of planning and implementing a nationwide vaccine campaign and producing a coherent strategy on how to use European funds cleverly obtained by the Conte II executive.

b) Second, Meloni, once again, in a zero-sum game (Albertazzi and Zulianello, 2022, Bruno, 2022b), was able to highlight and emphasize differences with Salvini's Lega (and to a lesser extent, FI, increasingly in decline, according to opinion polls at the time.) Notably, the Lega, an allied party but also the main opponent, was the big loser of the positioning of FdI, which cleverly managed to emerge as the real winner in the competition between PRRPs or far-right parties in Italy, depending on the definition we want to use[94].

---

[94] An account by Bruno and Parsi drafted in May 2021 noted the following: "The support of Forza Italia, creature of the former prime minister Silvio Berlusconi, was not a big surprise. But the decision by Matteo Salvini, an anti-immigration and often Euroskeptic radical-right populist, to commit his Lega to back the former ECB technocrat, was unexpected. Salvini claimed he would 'rather prefer to play the game and manage 209 billions of euros than not'. Yet in Budapest he recently met the prime ministers of Hungary and Poland, Viktor Orbán and Mateusz Morawiecki respectively. In November 2020, they had jeopardised the complex intergovernmental dynamics behind agreement on Next Generation EU — concerned that the rule-of-law mechanism attached to the stimulus would make it easier for Brussels to sanction violations of democratic principles. With the decision to support Draghi's executive, Salvini has opted to tie electoral support for the Lega to the long-term success of the PNRR. By contrast, the leader of Fratelli d'Italia, Giorgia Meloni, is betting on its failure and on the incapacity of the Draghi government to resolve the pandemic, alongside the economic situation, anytime soon. The Lega is now polling at around 22 per cent, with Fratelli d'Italia following at around 17.5 per cent (respectively 8 per cent down and 4.5 per cent up since the beginning of the pandemic). So the chances are high that the fate of the PNRR may decide the leadership of the center-right administration." (Bruno and Parsi, 2021).

Even with the Draghi government and throughout 2021, FdI continued to rise, according to opinion polls, at the expense of the parties supporting the executive led by the former ECB president[95]. After Sergio Mattarella's seven-year term, the issue of electing a new head of state in Italy arose in late 2021 or early 2022. This situation caused no small amount of discomfort in Italian parties, which

---

[95] Ever since the party led by Giorgia Meloni began to rapidly climb the political opinion polls, roughly in early 2020, coinciding with the spread of the COVID-19 pandemic, to establish itself as the leading political party in Italy, the issue of the cumbersome historical and political legacy of fascism has resurfaced. Initially, in a sporadic way, with few articles, then in a more and more systematic manner, at least until the month of October 2021, which can be considered as a sort of catalyst regarding the "explosion" of the old debated question of neo-fascism in Italy. As Bruno, Downes and Scopelliti (Bruno et al., 2021), among others, have pointed out, in the month of October 2021 at least three serious episodes have contributed to what can be defined as "the vexed question" of Italian politics: "… Italian politics has been shaken by recent events surrounding neo-fascism. Giorgia Meloni's radical right Fratelli d'Italia (Brothers of Italy) party has been adopting an ambiguous stance on the issue of neo-fascism, with Meloni failing to distance her party from these recent events. This has sparked a furore in Italy and at the same time raises important questions about the (a) legacy of fascism within modern Italian politics, particularly with (b) the increasing political significance that radical right parties such as the Brothers of Italy Party have alongside broader right-wing movements in contemporary Italian politics. In recent weeks, Italy has witnessed a series of disturbing events united by the resurgence of issues related to neo-fascism. First, an academic at the University of Bologna, Professor Andrea Morrone was recorded and accused of having labeled the Brothers of Italy party, led by Giorgia Meloni, as "fascist" or "neo-fascist", provoking the wrath of the party's MPs, who are now seeking to open a parliamentary debate on what happened. Subsequently, an Italian newspaper, Fanpage, revealed the results of a long investigation named "Lobby Nera", conducted through a journalist who infiltrated top circles of the radical-right and extreme-right wing in Milan, in particular related to Brothers of Italy. Crucially, this led to the discovery of a number of members of the Fratelli d'Italia party, including a member of the European Parliament Carlo Fidanza, who praised Adolf Hitler and anti-Semitism. Furthermore, Fidanza also displayed the Roman salute and made direct fun of Paolo Berizzi, a journalist of La Republica, famous for his important investigations and books against neo-fascist groups and movements, and currently the only journalist in Europe under escort for neo-Nazi threats. Most recently, on the 9th October in Rome, a no-vax demonstration of people against the green-pass certification led by the extreme right-wing neo-fascist party Forza Nuova (New Force) attacked the headquarters of the main Italian trade union, the Italian General Confederation of Labour (CGIL), completely devastating it. This latest event caused great shock in Italy and led to the subsequent arrest of twelve people, including the two leaders of Forza Nuova, Roberto Fiore and Giuliano Castellino."

appear to be growingly vulnerable to public opinion. The only precedent was Giorgio Napolitano, who was re-elected as Italy's head of state at the end of January 2022 because the parties were unable to agree. After a challenging week, the parliament chose Mario Draghi as the republic's president for a second term, rejecting both Pier Ferdinando Casini and Casini's own bids. Seven hundred and fifty-nine lawmakers voted in favor of Mattarella. Faced with the risk of a new paralysis with uncertain outcomes, party leaders decided to sound out the head of state's readiness. It is important to report that in early 2022, for the first time, opinion polls began to admit as possible an overtaking of FdI against Lega for months, paired around 22%.

The Russian invasion of Ukraine and the war

A significant international event took place in Europe about three weeks after Mattarella's re-election: Russia's invasion of Ukraine on February 24, 2022. Mario Draghi, the prime minister, quickly established himself as a steadfast supporter of Ukraine, following the example set by NATO and the EU. However, the government coalition begins to exhibit significant cracks in the months that followed the war, cracks that, by early summer 2022, become persistent and disruptive. Bruno and Fazio (2023) conclude that this support, included in the larger framework of meeting the NATO target of 2% of GDP for defense, could be considered the cause of the Draghi executive crisis. In addition, the increase in the defense budget certainly constituted an important element of friction between some government parties, in particular, the M5S; however, the Draghi government's crisis cannot be traced back to this alone[96].

The positioning of right-wing Italian political parties (FdI, Lega and FI) vis-à-vis the war in Ukraine during the Draghi executive has some interesting differences:

---

[96] Italy's support for Ukraine in relation to the conflict triggered by Russia has been very controversial and has inflamed public debate. In particular, the debate on Italy's military support to Ukraine continues to be battleground territory, often without the use of solid data and evidence, between majority and opposition political forces.

(i) FdI had pledged in favor of Ukraine's military and economic support, being in favor of sanctions against Russia throughout Mario Draghi's government (when it was the only party in opposition). From the beginning of the Russian invasion of Ukraine, Meloni had indicated that FdI fitted fully into the shared line drawn by the European institutions and NATO. In March 2022, Meloni said: "An unacceptable aggression has been made against Ukraine... It is right for the Italian government to remain united with the allies and move with them. On arms, I remember that the Latins used to say that if you want peace you must prepare for war. The government is doing well, we have approved what has been done so far. Even if the executive is not proving to be listened to internationally. Draghi continues to be excluded"[97]. However, it is important to note that the strongly pro-NATO and pro-EU stance of FdI has sometimes been viewed with suspicion in Italy and abroad, as on some occasions, Meloni and other party members had not hidden their admiration of Putin[98].

(ii) Lega is the party that has maintained the most ambiguous positioning with respect to support for Ukraine and condemnation of the war unleashed by Russia[99]. Salvini and colleagues have, on many occasions, stated that they do not view favorably both Italy's sending of arms to Ukraine and its support for sanctions against Russia. In May 2022, Salvini said, "I have talked about ceasefire and

---

[97] Notizie.it (11 March 2022) Guerra Ucraina, Meloni: "Giusto mandare le armi come supporto". https://www.notizie.it/guerra-ucraina-meloni-giusto-mand are-le-armi-come-supporto/.

[98] For instance, in her autobiography, Meloni states (Meloni, 2021: 317): "… but Russia is part of our European value system, defends Christian identity and fights Islamic fundamentalism". In this chapter all translations from Italian have been produced by the authors. Originally: "… ma la Russia è parte del nostro sistema di valori europei, difende l'identità cristiana e combatte il fondamentalismo islamico".

[99] The proximity of the Salvini-led party with Putin, his political party (United Russia) and his power circles is a topic that continues to be much debated despite some evidences, particularly concerning fundings for the Lega. See for instance Stampa (5 September 2022) L'accordo Salvini-Mosca: ecco cosa c'è dietro alle posizioni leghiste in campagna elettorale https://www.lastampa.it/polit ica/2022/09/05/news/laccordo_salvinimosca_ecco_cosa_ce_dietro_alle_posi zioni_leghiste_in_campagna_elettorale-8433608/.

disarmament, so these go by a stop of sending weapons".[100] In fact, Salvini, in those days, had repeatedly discussed with then PM Draghi, expressing disagreement on sending Italian arms to Ukraine, in his view, without success. There have also been some clashes with ally FdI regarding sanctions against Russia. During the election campaign in September 2022, Salvini had expressed, provoking dry remarks from Meloni, the belief that "'Sanctions are fuelling the war'. Many businessmen are asking me to review them. The Italians are losing out and the Russians are gaining, so in Brussels there is someone who has miscalculated," and, still on sanctions, "They are not working, rethinking the strategy is essential to save jobs and businesses in Italy".[101]

(iii) Lastly, FI's positioning vis-à-vis the issue of support for Ukraine has always been controversial. Statements by party president Berlusconi often diverged from the party's official line, with numerous 'corrections' by the party coordinator Antonio Tajani or communications officers, often justifying it as phrases being analyzed 'out of context'. The EPP has found itself forced, on numerous occasions, to have to reiterate, also on social media and with much embarrassment, the alignment of FI and Berlusconi with its own positions[102] or even showing satisfaction with FI's election result, confident that it "Forza Italia will guide the next government into a path that serves the best interests of the Italian people as part of a strong and stable Europe".[103] On one hand, on almost every occasion concerning the vote in parliament, FI has supported the government led by Draghi. On the other hand, in May 2022, Berlusconi clearly stated, "We have no leaders in the world, we have no leaders in Europe. One world leader who was supposed to approach Putin at the mediation table called him a war criminal and said he had to leave the Russian government. Another, NATO secretary, said that

---

[100] Adnkronos (16 May 2022) Ucraina, Salvini: 'Stop a invio armi, l'ho detto a Draghi' https://www.adnkronos.com/ucraina-salvini-stop-a-invio-armi-lho-detto-a-draghi_1xGKJAP5YBINXDh0QCovWT.
[101] Repubblica (4 September 2022) Salvini contro le sanzioni, Meloni lo gela: "Non saremo l'anello debole con Mosca" https://www.repubblica.it/politica/2022/09/04/news/salvini_sanzioni_russia-364111866/.
[102] https://twitter.com/EPP/status/1573250122200276994.
[103] https://twitter.com/epp/status/1574344617817948160.

the independence of the Donbas would never be recognized [[...]] You understand that with these promises, Mr. Putin is far from sitting at a table".[104]

The Draghi government crisis of July 2022 was triggered by an increasing struggle with the M5S party[105] in relation to a number of dossiers, including military support for Ukraine and the annual defense budget, it is undeniable that both FI and the Lega themselves contributed to the downfall of the government headed by the former president of the European Central Bank, saying that they would no longer support a government also formed by the M5S, leading to snap election in September 2022[106].

---

[104] Sky (17 May 2022) Ucraina, Berlusconi: "Italia è in guerra perché sta inviando armi a Kiev" https://tg24.sky.it/politica/2022/05/17/guerra-ucraina-berlusconi-armi.

[105] M5S is the Italian party that more fiercely has disagreed on supporting Ukraine with weapons, both during the Draghi and the current Meloni executive. As Bruno (2022b: 168-169; see also Bruno and Cozzolino, 2022 and Fazio and Bruno, 2023) has pointed out, until the resignation of Draghi in July 2022, the party led by former PM Giuseppe Conte had, since September 2019, been in an alliance with the PD that saw the two parties form a government (Conte cabinet II), and later supporting the Draghi executive. In this period, the ideological stance of the M5S had seemingly shifted from ideologically ambiguous populist positions to pro-EU, moderate and liberal positioning. In particular, this shift, strongly supported by at the time foreign minister Luigi Di Maio, seemed to hold firm until the debate on arming Ukraine following Russia's invasion in late February 2022. In fact, the political willingness of the executive branch to arm Ukraine inflamed discussions over defense investments and increases to the country's defense budget. On 21 June, Di Maio quit the M5S: the *casus belli* was indeed the supply of arms to Ukraine and, more generally, Italy's international positioning, namely its support for NATO and recent EU decisions which had, according to Di Maio, been insufficiently supported by the M5S, currently led by Giuseppe Conte. Earlier, in spring 2022, a heated debate among the political forces supporting the government led by Draghi took place. Draghi appeared rather appalled (going as far as to inform Italian President Sergio Mattarella) by the remarks made by Conte, who argued against increasing the Italian defense budget at a point when the country was still grappling with the COVID-19 health crisis and its socio-economic fall-out. Subsequently as we have seen, for various reasons (related both to local situations and Italy's international positioning), a government crisis was triggered, first by the M5S hesitations and then by Lega and Forza Italia's lack of confidence in the Draghi executive, leading de facto to election in September 2022.

[106] Rai News (16 July 2022) Diario della crisi. Riunito il consiglio nazionale del Movimento Cinque Stelle https://www.rainews.it/maratona/2022/07/diario-della-crisi-riunito-il-consiglio-nazionale-del-movimento-5-stelle-ed97a659-c911-4f68-bc24-c6e20131ab97.html.

Conclusion

Therefore, this chapter analyzed the first decade of the life of the FdI party, starting from the foundation in late 2012 up to the current day, with Giorgia Meloni serving as Italy's PM. As we have seen, relatively unnoticed, FdI was founded in December 2012 by Meloni, La Russa (former members of AN dissolved in 2009), and Crosetto during the *crisi dello spread* involving the fourth and last Berlusconi cabinet (2008-2011), in the framework of the broader European sovereign debt crisis, a multi-year debt crisis that took place in the EU from 2009. The three, who did not follow Gianfranco Fini in his new political project, decided to secede from Berlusconi's Il Popolo della Libertà, unhappy, among other things, about his support to the technocratic executive led by Mario Monti, the former EU commissioner. In a decade, roughly from late 2011 up to 2022, FdI managed to evolve from a small party in danger of disappearing (according to its founder, Meloni) to be the first in Italy, resulting in the undisputed winner of the September 25 Italian general election, with around 26% of the preferences, leading a right-wing coalition that obtained around 44% of the votes overall (Chiaramonte and De Sio, 2024).

References

Aït-Aoudia, M, et al. (2011). The Genesis of Political Parties: An Analysis of the Front National, the Movimento Sociale Italiano and the Islamic Salvation Front. *Revue Française de Science Politique* (English Edition).

Albertazzi, D., and McDonnell, D. (2005). The Lega Nord in the second Berlusconi government: In a league of its own. *West European Politics, 28*(5), 952-972.

Albertazzi, D., and McDonnell, D. (2010). The Lega Nord back in government. *West European Politics, 33*(6), 1318-1340.

Albertazzi, D., and Zulianello, M. (2022). Italy's election is a case study in a new phase for the radical right. *The Conversation*. Available at: https://theconversation.com/italys-election-is-a-case-study-in-a-new-phase-for-the-radical-right-92198

Albertazzi, D., Bonansinga, A. and Zulianello, M. (2021). The right-wing alliance at the time of the Covid-19 pandemic: all change?. *Contemporary Italian Politics 13:2*, 181-195.

Albertazzi, D., Giovannini, A., and Seddone, A. (2018). 'No regionalism please, we are Leghisti!' The transformation of the Italian Lega Nord under the leadership of Matteo Salvini. *Regional & Federal Studies*, 28(5), 645-671.

Alonzi, R. (2020). Searching for the EU Political Identity: Experience of the Italian Yellow-Green Government (2018-2019). *RUDN Journal of Political Science*, 22(1), 92-104.

Bickerton, C. J., and Accetti, C. I. (2018). Techno-populism'as a new party family: the case of the Five Star Movement and Podemos. *Contemporary Italian Politics*, 10(2), 132-150.

Bruno, V. A. and Fazio, F. (2023). Italian governments and political parties vis-à-vis the war in Ukraine. In Anja Mihr and Chiara Pierobon (Eds.), *Polarization, Shifting Borders and Liquid Governance: Studies on Transformation and Development in the OSCE Region* (pp. 265-283). OSCE Academy in Bishkek (Kyrgyzstan), Springer.

Bruno, V. A. and Parsi, V. E. (2021, 13 May). Can Italy's center-right coalition recover from far-right influence? *Social Europe*. Available at: https://socialeurope.eu/can-italys-center-right-coalition-recover-from-far-right-influence.

Bruno, V. A. (2018). The Production of Fear. European Democracies in the Age of Populisms and Technocracies. *Social Europe Journal*, 13 June 2018. From: https://socialeurope.eu/the-production-of-fear-europe an-democracies-inthe- age-of-populisms-and-technocracies.

Bruno, V. A. (2020) Between Scylla and Charybdis: Technocratic and Populist Fears Compressing Liberal Democracies. In Feix, M., Thiel, M., Dembinski, P. H. (Eds.), *Peuple et populisme, identité et nation. Quelle contribution à la paix? Quelles perspectives européenne?*, (pp. 147- 158). Strasbourg: Presses Universitaires de Strasbourg.

Bruno, V. A. (2021, 1 March). The Italian Far-right's Long-Term Investment. *Fair Observer*. Available at: https://www.radicalrightanalysis.com/2021/03/16/the-italian-far-rights-long-term-investment/

Bruno, V. A. (2022). Online use of Slogans, Symbols and Slurs by the Italian Radical Right. In *Symbols & Slogans of the Radical Right Online: Italy, Germany, France* (Vol. 2022, No. A, 2-64). ACS. Available at: https://www.academicconsulting.co.uk/_files/ugd/4775ea_eb523462f5cb43beb4c72dadbce90ee1.pdf?index=true

Bruno, V. A. (2022b). 'Center right? What center right?' Italy's right-wing coalition: Forza Italia's political 'heritage' and the mainstreaming of the far-right. In V. A. Bruno (Ed.), *Populism and Far-Right. Trends in Europe* (pp. 163-195). Milan: EDUCatt.

Bruno, V. A., and Downes, J. F. (2020b). COVID-19 and the (temporary) fall of the populist radical right in European politics?. In T. Bar-On, & B. Molas (Eds.) *Radical Right-Wing Responses to COVID-19*. Stuttgart: Ibidem-Verlag.

Bruno, V. A., and Downes, J. F. (2018, 23 October). Is Italy's Populist Government Manufacturing The Next Political Crisis? *Social Europe*. Available at: https://socialeurope.eu/is-italys-populist-governmen t-manufacturing-the-next-political-crisis.

Bruno, V. A., and Downes, J. F. (2020). The case of Fratelli d'Italia: how radical-right populists in and beyond are building global networks. *Democratic Audit Blog*.

Bruno, V. A., and Finzi, G. (2018). Leading through a Decade of Crisis — Not Bad, After All: Germany's Leadership Demand and Followership Inclusion, 2008-2018. *German Politics and Society*, 36(4), 50-77.

Bruno, V. A., Downes, J. F. and Scopelliti, A. (2020, 14 October). The Aftermath of the Constitutional Referendum in Italy: Stability for the Conte Executive, Lega on the decline and Fratelli d'Italia on the rise? *CARR Insight blog*. Available at: https://www.radicalrightanalysis. com/2020/10/14/the-aftermath-of-the-constitutional-referendum-in-italy-stability-for-the-conte-executive-lega-on-the-decline-fratelli-ditalia-on-the-rise/

Bruno, V. A., Downes, J. F. and Scopelliti, A. (2021, 12 November). Post-Fascism in Italy: "So why this flame, Mrs. Giorgia Meloni?". *Culturico*. Available at: https://culturico.com/2021/11/12/post-fascis m-in-italy-so-why-this-flame-mrs-giorgia-meloni/.

Bull, A. C., and Gilbert, M. (2001). *The Lega Nord and the northern question in Italian politics*. Houndmills & New York: Palgrave.

Castelli Gattinara, P., and Froio, C. (2021). Italy: the Mainstream Right and its Allies, 1994-2018. In T. Bale and C. Rovira Kaltwasser (Eds.)., *Riding the Populist Wave. Europe's Mainstream Right in Crisis*. Cambridge: Cambridge University Press.

Chiaramonte, A. and De Sio, L. (Eds.) (2024). *Un polo solo. Le elezioni politiche del 2022*. Bologna: Il Mulino.

Cozzolino, A. (2019). Reconfiguring the state: Executive powers, emergency legislation, and neoliberalization in Italy. *Globalizations*, 16(3), 336-352.

De Luca, R., and Fruncillo, D. (2019). La Lega "nazionale" di Salvini alla conquista elettorale del Meridione. *Italian Journal of Electoral Studies IJES-QOE*, 82(2), 49-84.

Donà, A. (2022). The rise of the Radical Right in Italy: the case of Fratelli d'Italia. *Journal of Modern Italian Studies*, 27 (5), 775-794.

Downes, J. F. (2020, 24 September). How the far-right took over the mainstream. openDemocracy. Available at: https://www.opendemocracy.net/en/countering-radical-right/how-far-right-took-over-mainstream/

Fratelli d'Italia (2017). Le Tesi di Trieste per il movimento dei patrioti. From https://www.fratelli-italia.it/le-tesi-trieste/

Fratelli d'Italia (2022). Il Programma. Pronti a risollevare l'Italia. From https://www.fratelli-italia.it/programma/.

Giannetti, D., Pinto, L., and Plescia, C. (2020). The first Conte government: 'government of change' or business as usual? *Contemporary Italian Politics*, 12(2), 182-199.

Ignazi, P. (1994). *L'estrema destra in Europa*. Bologna: Il Mulino.

Leidig, E. (Ed.) (2020). *The Mainstreaming the Global Radical Right*. Stuttgart: Ibidem-Verlag.

Meloni, G. (2021). *Io sono Giorgia. Le mie radici, le mie idee*. Milano: Rizzoli.

Mosca, L. (2014). The five star movement: exception or vanguard in Europe? *The International Spectator*, 49(1), 36-52.

Mosca, L., and Tronconi, F. (2019). Beyond left and right: the eclectic populism of the Five Star Movement. *West European Politics*, 42(6), 1258-1283.

Mudde, C. (2019). *The far-right today*. Hoboken: John Wiley & Sons.

Mudde, C. (2021). Populism in Europe: An Illiberal Democratic Response to Undemocratic Liberalism (The Government and Opposition/Leonard Schapiro Lecture 2019). *Government and Opposition, 1-21*.

Passarelli, G., and Tuorto, D. (2018). The Five Star Movement: Purely a matter of protest? The rise of a new party between political discontent and reasoned voting. *Party Politics*, 24(2), 129-140.

Passarelli, G. and Tuorto, D. (2018b). *La Lega di Salvini Estrema destra di governo*. Bologna: Il Mulino.

Pirro, A. L. (2018). The polyvalent populism of the 5 Star Movement. *Journal of Contemporary European Studies*, 26(4), 443-458.

Rai News (2014, 9 March). *Meloni: "Noi la destra popolare, Italia fuori dall'Euro"*. Available at: https://www.rainews.it/dl/rainews/articoli/meloni-italia-no-euro-noi-destra-popolare-544a1a84-53aa-4d1a-b3fd-4c820b7dccd7.html

Repubblica (2020, 22 April). Dieci anni fa il "Che fai, mi cacci?" di Fini a Berlusconi. La Russa: "Avrei seguito Gianfranco, ma era diventato di centro". From https://www.corriere.it/video-articoli/2020/04/22/dieci-anni-fa-che-fai-mi-cacci-fini-berlusconi-russa-avrei-seguito-gianfranco-ma-era-diventato-centro/c0481566-8474-11ea-8d8e-1dff96ef3536.shtml.

Repubblica (2022, 15 October). Ignazio La Russa e Lorenzo Fontana, presidenti che dividono. Fromishttps://www.repubblica.it/commenti/2022/10/15/news/fontana_camera_la_russa_senato_governo_meloni-370077580/

Schwörer, J. and Fernández-García, B., (2021). Demonisation of political discourses? How mainstream parties talk about the populist radical right. *West European Politics 44* (7), 1401-1424.

Tarchi, M. (2003) The Lega Nord. In L. De Winter and H. Tursan (Eds.). *Regionalist parties in Western Europe* (pp. 161–175). London: Routledge.

Tooze, A. (2018). *Crashed: How a Decade of Financial Crises Changed the World.* London: Viking

Tronconi, F. (Ed.). (2015). *Beppe Grillo's Five Star Movement: Organisation, Communication and Ideology.* London: Ashgate Publishing, Ltd.

Valbruzzi, M. (2018). When populists meet technocrats. The Italian innovation in government formation. *Journal of Modern Italian Studies, 23*(4), 460-480.

Vampa, D. (2015). Local representative democracy and protest politics: the case of the Five-star Movement. *Contemporary Italian Politics, 7*(3), 232-250.

Wondreys, J., and Mudde, C. (2020). Victims of the Pandemic? European Far-Right Parties and COVID-19. *Nationalities Papers,* 1-18. doi:10.1017/nps.2020.93.

YouTrend (12 November 2021). *Supermedia dei sondaggi politici: crescono PD e M5S.* Available at: https://www.youtrend.it/2021/11/12/supermedia-dei-sondaggi-politici-crescono-pd-e-m5s

Chapter 5
Electoral Volatility: The Post-2018 Electoral Decline of the Valence Populist M5S Party in Italy[107]

This chapter explores the context of electoral volatility in Italian politics by examining the electoral decline of the populist Italian Five Star Movement (M5S) after the 2018 Italian general election. Italian politics has often been characterized by its high levels of electoral volatility, with Italy having an astonishing 69 governments in the post-war period (since 1945). This chapter finds that M5S self-sabotaged its electoral prospects due to the (a) resulting anti-incumbency effects from its recent governing experiences and due to (b) intraparty ideological and organizational factors. M5S's ideological ambiguity and catch-all nature, alongside internal division, have hindered the party electorally in recent years, (c) increasing internal party factions (dissent) over ideological issues and (d) the 'clear' (clarity) stances adopted by their right-wing electoral competitors, in the form of Lega and FdI. Though M5S has been in a coalition government and served in three successive terms, the electoral future of M5S looks increasingly uncertain.

In the latest legislature (preceding the October 2022 Italian general election) three different governing coalitions determined the formation of three distinct governments (i.e., Conte I, Conte II and Draghi Cabinets), all with the support of the populist M5S party (Movimento 5 Stelle—M5S), whose electoral fortunes, ideological features and interparty behavior has been examined by a significant branch of scholarly research (see Conti and Memoli, 2015; Franzosi et al., 2015; Pedrazzani and Pinto, 2013).

Since the party was founded, M5S has focused on anti-establishment stances, on the merit of direct democracy alongside the

---

[107] The authors would like to especially thank Nicola Palma (University of Bologna) for providing excellent research and data support for this accompanying chapter.

need for redistributive and environmental policies (see Pirro, 2018). From an electoral perspective, M5S rose to prominence in Italian politics in the 2013 Italian general election, when it secured the highest electoral support among all Italian political parties. At the subsequent 2018 national parliamentary election, the party confirmed its electoral rise, becoming the first-placed party and entering a coalition government with the populist radical right League Party (Lega—L)[108].

In fact, despite having increased its votes by over two million compared to the previous political elections in 2013, the M5S did not obtain the required majority to form a government and negotiated a coalition arrangement with its radical right electoral competitor. The governing coalition with the League lasted only one year until 2019, with a second coalition government being formed between the M5S and the 'mainstream' left-wing Democratic Party (Partito Democratico—PD). In 2021, after the fall of the Conte II cabinet, M5S supported the formation of the technocratic government chaired by Prime Minister Mario Draghi (Draghi Cabinet, 2021–2022).

Nonetheless, despite having achieved the highest roles in government, the M5S party experienced a significant reduction in its overall vote share in a recent second-order election (2019 European Parliament election) alongside recent third-order elections (regional elections in 2019 and 2020), continuing to experience a significant electoral decline in the polls post-2018 Italian general election. Conversely, the Italian center-right coalition has now arguably shifted toward a fully-fledged radical-right coalition, with the PRRPs, the League led by Matteo Salvini and Brothers of Italy (Fratelli d'Italia—FdI) led by Giorgia Meloni, becoming increasingly influential in Italian politics at both the regional and national levels.[109]

The existing populism literature has examined the electoral decline and failures of populist radical right parties in recent years,

---

[108] The Source of the 2013 and 2018 Italian General Elections: http://elezionistorico.interno.it/index.php?tpel=C&dtel.

[109] We use the terms 'populist radical right', 'radical right' and 'far-right' interchangeably throughout this chapter, when referring to the League (L) and Brothers of Italy (FdI) Parties.

spanning the Benelux countries (de Jonge, 2021), Belgium (de Jonge, 2020; Pauwels, 2011), the Netherlands (De Lange & Art, 2011) and Austria (Luther, 2011). Heinisch's (2003) seminal study investigated populist radical right parties' failures in government and drew on the case of the Freedom Party of Austria alongside populist radical right parties in both the Italian and Dutch political contexts.

While extensive research in recent years has been conducted in the literature on the electoral fortunes and failures of populist radical right parties, much less is known about the case of other types (i.e., more unique) forms of populist parties, such as the case of the M5S Party in the Italian political context. This chapter aims to fill this important gap in the literature by examining the main explanations surrounding the electoral decline of the valence populist M5S party in the post-2018 Italian general election,

The Italian case study represents a unique political context characterized by an ideologically ambiguous populist party in power, which is currently experiencing a drastic electoral decline and marked by a complex pattern of party competition with rising partisan dealignment trends and high levels of political distrust.

To examine the electoral decline of the M5S Party within the context of electoral volatility in Italian politics, this chapter examines data from the party level of analysis. This chapter draws on the Chapel Hill Expert Survey (CHES) alongside regional parties' performance data. It seeks to build up a comprehensive picture for understanding the different factors that led to the recent electoral decline.

Defining populism and the case of the M5S

A wealth of academic research has been conducted on the concept of populism in recent years. There are numerous key features of populism: the antagonistic struggle between the 'pure people' and the corrupt elite, as well as a harsh criticism of the institutions of representative democracy (see Taggart, 2000; Mudde, 2004, 2007). These elements have characterized the political rise and the electoral success of the populist M5S Party in Italy. From the initial refusal to forge alliances with traditional political parties considered as belonging to a corrupt caste (see Corbetta and Gualmini, 2013) to the emphasis attributed to the tools of direct democracy, capable of involving citizens in the decision-making process (Manucci and Amsler, 2018); alongside post-ideological approaches capable of guaranteeing the electoral support of voters now disillusioned by the crisis of the political system (Russo et al., 2017).

This chapter builds on the existing literature in party politics, which argues that the M5S party should be defined as neither a left-wing political party nor a right one due to its capacity to adopt contingent stances located at different points in the ideological left-right spectrum. This approach is consistent with recent contributions to the study of populism, such as the *valence* populist classification (see Zulianello, 2020). Building on the so-called ideational approach to populism (Hawkins et al., 2019; Mudde, 2007), this categorization enriches the traditional distinction between left-wing and right-wing populist parties by adding a new variant to which valence populist parties belong.

Instead of being ideologically positioned along the various dimensions of the party system, valence populist parties emphasize non-positional policy domains, such as anti-corruption and anti-political establishment rhetoric. Furthermore, the pairing of populist rhetoric and a diversified ideological background also operates in the definitions of other scholars who identify as *polyvalent* or *eclectic* tendency of M5S to adopt left-wing positions on economic issues while adopting conservative positions on socio-cultural policy issues, such as the party's vague and nativist position on immigration and European integration (see Mosca and Tronconi, 2019; Pirro, 2018; Pirro and Taggart, 2018; Zulianello, 2020).

The party's diverse ideology also reflects the ideological and political positioning of its voters (see Isernia and Piccolino, 2018). The electoral success of M5S, especially its exceptional result achieved in the 2018 Italian general election, occurred in a political context of increasing dissatisfaction among voters with existing political parties in the mainstream of Italian politics, alongside socio-economic events like the long-term effects of multiple crises in Europe, such as the 2008–13 economic crisis (Downes and Loveless, 2018) and the 2015–2018 EU refugee crisis (Downes et al., 2021).

Since it was founded, M5S has focused on anti-establishment positions, on the merit of direct democracy alongside the need for redistributive and environmental policies. In particular, by means of emphasizing welfare and social protection policies, the party acted as issue-entrepreneurs to secure electoral consensus, exploiting the low emphasis attributed by mainstream parties to policy issues related to the provision of social welfare schemes (De Vries and Hobolt, 2014). Thus, prior to the 2018 Italian general election, the M5S centered its electoral propaganda on its anti-establishment rhetoric alongside the support of redistributive policies to reduce poverty and enhance social security schemes for unemployed persons.

The party also capitalized on voters' growing anti-immigrant and euro-skeptic stances, traditionally exploited by far-right parties. On the one hand, and not without a high degree of intra-party dissent, M5S sought to shift further right-wing on the socio-cultural issue dimension, arguably as a strategy to capture certain types of voters that demanded more restrictive measures to counter illegal immigration. On the other hand, M5S frequently criticized the EU leadership, outlining concerns about the risk of non-compliance with both budgetary and fiscal targets due to the enactment of redistributive policies in Italian politics (D'Alimonte, 2018; Chiaramonte and De Sio, 2019).

Theory

Regardless of whether electoral success allows a political party to form a government or, more broadly, to gain seats in the legislative assembly, political parties face the pressure of maintaining or enhancing their electoral performance in subsequent national or subnational elections (Van Haute and Pilet, 2006; Bolleyer et al., 2013). Following this strand of literature, Bolleyer and Bytzek (2016) have also highlighted the implications of parties' organizational factors, such as the capacity to rely on solid territorial bases, leadership stability, and parties' electoral performances. In addition, parties' involvement in the process of government formation will conceivably alter the electoral performance in the post-incumbency period (see

Uppal, 2009; Downes and Loveless, 2018) especially for those political parties that rose to prominence for their anti-establishment and anti-elite rhetoric (McDonnell and Newell, 2011).

In addition, intra-party features can alter the general electoral trajectory of political parties. Recent findings show how parties' internal division (see Lehrer and Lin, 2018; Plescia et al., 2020) and ambiguity (Tomz and Van Houweling, 2009; Brauninger and Giger, 2018) may influence intra-party politics and the overall parties' electoral performances. Somer-Topcu (2015) defines broad-appeal strategies as the electoral tactics that political parties implement to gain electoral consensus from an ideologically diversified electoral base. On the one hand, instead of being firmly positioned along the various dimensions of the party system and therefore being ideologically identifiable by the electorate on a specific side of the political spectrum, political parties may assume clear stances on both the left and the right, depending on what policy issues are being considered. On the other hand, political parties may adopt electoral and mass appeal strategies to disguise (i.e., *issue blurring*) their political positions for the electoral purpose of enlarging their political base (Rovny, 2012). Thus, instead of being ideologically clear (i.e., having *clarity),* this electoral strategy entails political parties and candidates with a tendency to assume vague stances on various policy issues (Shepsle, 1972).

Furthermore, intra-party conflict and division have an impact on the electoral fortunes of political parties. Recent findings show that parties' internal divisions undermine their electoral results (see Barrett, 2018; Greene and Haber, 2015), while other scholars highlight the existing linkage between parties' internal divisions and heterogeneity and the emphasis attributed to specific policy issues (see Spoon, 2012; Steiner and Mader, 2019). Furthermore, the parties' ideological and ambiguous natures and intra-party levels of dissent are not discrete aspects. In fact, Lin and Leherer (2020) show that the electoral strategy of assuming ambiguous stances is ineffective when voters have perceptions of an internally divided political party.

Thus, the Five Star Movement's electoral success in 2018 and the party's sharp electoral collapse in its vote share in almost all the regional elections after its participation in government represents an important case of a populist party in power with a high degree of intra-party dissent that subsequently experienced a drastic electoral decline. It is worthwhile examining the potential causes of its electoral failure after the party achieved a historic and significant electoral result at the 2018 Italian General Election.

This chapter argues that while M5S's ambiguity initially helped the party to break through at the national level by means of appealing to a heterogenous electorate (see Pirro, 2018), this same electoral strategy alongside the party's organizational features, such as its lack of an extra-parliamentary base at territorial level prevented M5S from achieving a further electoral consolidation in the subsequent sub-national elections and led to the party experiencing a substantial electoral decline. Conversely, the Five Star Movement's two distinct previous coalition partners, the League (2018–2019) and the Democratic Party (2019–2021), which have tended to adopt clearer and more identifiable positions in the eyes of the electorate, achieved stronger and more positive electoral results.

This chapter adopts a party-level approach to investigate further the combined electoral decline of the M5S across a wider timeframe which also considers the broader electoral rise of both the radical right League and Brothers of Italy political parties. Thus, this chapter sets out to investigate whether changes in ideological positioning, whose significant breadth can be interpreted as ideological ambiguity, combined with the degree of intra-party party dissent, have played a role in explaining the electoral decline of the M5S in the post-2018 Italian general election political landscape.

Research design

The methodology in this chapter makes use of the CHES data (2014 and 2019 waves) alongside recent regional electoral performance data of different political parties. This chapter relies on specific features of political parties (i.e., ideological positioning and degree of intra-party dissent) derived from the CHES expert surveys to highlight the potential causes of the electoral decline experienced by

M5S after its government agreement with the radical right League party in 2018. This empirical strategy is part of a broader framework that analyzes parties' electoral performances in Italian politics and changes in parties' vote shares from data collected at the regional level of analysis for the period between 2014 and 2020. More specifically, this chapter collects parties' performance data for regional elections that took place after the 2018 Italian general election and the subsequent first coalition agreement.

The focus on Italian regional elections post-2018 general election provides us with the most accurate measure to fully capture the electoral decline of M5S and the main factors behind it. This chapter investigates the extent to which M5S's change in policy positions (i.e., the issue blurring strategy), alongside the degree of intra-party dissent on the key policy dimensions that are meaningful for the electorate, might explain its electoral decline.

Empirical analysis

In the next section this chapter analyzes the significant electoral decline of M5S in regional elections post the 2018 coalition government agreement. The chapter then investigates the extent to which the combination of external factors (i.e., significant change in policy positions) and internal party features (i.e., intra-party dissent) contributes to explaining the decline in electoral fortunes for M5S at the regional level.

Regional electoral performance

This chapter examines the key regional-level findings in our chapter. Table 5.1 demonstrates the significant electoral decline experienced by M5S (2019–2020). The chapter collects party performance data for all the regional elections that took place after the M5S's coalition government agreement in 2018 (t-1). We computed the percentage change in vote shares between the first regional election after the 2018 Italian general election and the first regional election before 2018. We only focus on those political parties which exceeded the three per cent minimum threshold for party representation in the 2018 Italian general election. For all the examined electoral rounds, the chapter finds evidence of a significant electoral decline in voters' support toward M5S, coinciding with its experience in the two recent governing coalitions, with both the radical right League (i.e., the Conte I Cabinet) and the left-wing Democratic Party (i.e., the Conte II Cabinet). Furthermore, the electoral success of its right-wing competitors has been shown to be particularly strong, even in historically traditional left-wing regions, such as the Northern Italian region of Emilia-Romagna.

The results of the post-2018 regional elections show that despite the 2018 general election success of the Five Star Movement at the national level, the wider regional level analysis depicts a bleak picture for the party. Moreover, the electorate at the regional level is divided between the support toward left-wing and right-wing coalitions, especially in the form of increasing support toward the radical right League party. The explanations for M5S's electoral decline at the regional level are multifaceted. These explanations range from the lack of a clear organizational structure at the subnational level to the attitudes of the M5S leadership hierarchy, struggling with different internal factions and political currents, alongside the resignation of Luigi Di Maio as the leader of the party in early 2020. Furthermore, the M5S party and its leadership hierarchy had to come to terms with the increasing perception that the party was no longer an insurgent anti-establishment 'challenger' party but instead is now effectively part of the political establishment as a 'governing' party, having served in the last three coalition governments.

Table 5.1: Changes in Vote Shares for Selected Parties (2014–2020) at the Regional Level

Election	Regions	Political Parties				
		Five Star Movement	The League[110]	Brothers of Italy	Democratic Party	Forward Italy
February 2019	Abruzzo	-1.25 (↓)	*	3.54 (↑)	-14.37 (↓)	-7.65 (↓)
March 2019	Basilicata	11.3 (↑)	*	0.82 (↑)	-17.09 (↓)	-3.13 (↓)
May 2019	Piemonte	-7.8 (↓)	29.83 (↑)	1.75 (↑)	-13.73 (↓)	-7.15 (↓)
October 2019	Umbria	-7.15 (↓)	22.96 (↑)	4.16 (↑)	-13.43 (↓)	-3.03 (↓)
January 2020	Calabria	1.37 (↑)	*	8.38 (↑)	-8.48 (↓)	0.06 (↑)
January 2020	Emilia-Romagna	-8.53 (↓)	12.53 (↑)	6.67 (↑)	-9.84 (↓)	-5.8 (↓)
September 2020	Campania	-7.1 (↓)	*	0.51 (↑)	-2.59 (↓)	-12.66 (↓)
September 2020	Liguria	-14.51 (↓)	-3.11 (↓)	7.8 (↑)	-5.75 (↓)	-7.39 (↓)
September 2020	Marche	-11.77 (↓)	9.36 (↑)	12.15 (↑)	-10.02 (↓)	-3.51 (↓)
September 2020	Puglia	-7.33 (↓)	7.15 (↑)	10.18 (↑)	-2.55 (↓)	-2.46 (↓)
September 2020	Toscana	-7.99 (↓)	5.76 (↑)	9.68 (↑)	-11.24 (↓)	-4.13 (↓)
September 2020	Veneto	-7.72 (↓)	-0.91 (↓)	2.6 (↑)	-4.74 (↓)	-2.41 (↓)

Notes: *denotes that the change in vote shares cannot be calculated (t-1) Source: Authors' Data of recent Regional Election Performances.

In the 2018 Italian general election, M5S became the single biggest party in Italian politics, challenging the traditional mainstream center-left (Democratic Party) and center-right (Forward Italy) parties.

---

[110] Asterisks (*) denote those regions for which it is not possible to make a comparison of the regional election results for the League, since the party did not participate in the regional election that took place prior the general election in 2018.

ELECTORAL VOLATILITY 149

Recent regional elections also demonstrated a significant electoral decline for M5S, alongside increased levels of support for the two radical right parties (The League and The Brothers of Italy Parties). The reasons for M5S's electoral debacle are multifaceted. Compared to a number of traditional mainstream parties, M5S lacks distinct regional roots. M5S also lacks local entrenchment, with the nature of regional elections often offering greater chances of defeat for those parties that do not have a solid territorial base. At the same time, M5S may have also lost its uniqueness (i.e., the party's status as an 'outsider'/populist party) now that it has served in the last three coalition governments (i.e., become part of the ruling establishment) at the national level.

Furthermore, the attitude of the M5S leadership and its weak internal cohesion has led the party to refuse any coalition agreement in some regional elections, while in other regions, M5S has teamed up with the former government ally, the Democratic Party (the Conte I Cabinet). The M5S is struggling with different internal factions and political currents that also reflect the diversified nature of its target electorate. Part of M5S's voters did not arguably foresee a governing alliance with the radical right League. In contrast, others expected the former government's agreement with the Democratic Party to become structural and long-term oriented under the leadership of former President Giuseppe Conte.

On the other hand, we argue in this chapter that the ambiguous nature of the party and the tendency to change its positions on key issue dimensions has clearly affected the party's electoral performance. Indeed, while the party's radical right competitors, the League and Brothers of Italy, have adopted clearer positions on a wide range of socio-cultural issues, the party's ideologically ambiguous nature has arguably made it difficult for its policies to resonate clearly among Italian voters.

Party positions

A party-level analysis does not intend to offer deterministic conclusions but rather to provide an exploratory study of the potential factors behind M5S's pronounced regional electoral decline post the

2018 coalition agreement. Based on the empirical findings of the electoral support model outlined above (Table 1), the chapter explores independent variables, the policy issues that appear to be significant for the M5S's electorate in defining its electoral support toward the party, the socioeconomic policy dimension related to redistribution policies and the socio-cultural dimension of electoral support related to immigration-related issues.[111]

Relying on the CHES expert survey, we consider the change in parties' policy positions that occur between one regional election and the other (i.e., the 2014 and 2019 waves) and the actual degree of intra-party dissent on economic and cultural issues (i.e., the 2019 wave). Parties' positions on immigration, alongside their economic orientation toward redistributive policies, are measured on a 10-point scale. A score of 10 stands for a more restrictive and anti-immigrant stance, whereas a score of 0 implies a more positive attitude toward immigration. Regarding the economic dimension of electoral support, a score of 0 implies that a political party favors state intervention in reducing differences in income levels, whereas a score of 10 implies that a party strongly opposes redistribution measures.

The results show that low levels of intra-party dissent affect the economic dimension of electoral support to a greater extent than the cultural dimension. In particular, high levels of internal division on economic-redistributive issues reduce the probability that a party has improved its electoral performance in the regional elections after 2018, regardless of the change in the parties' policy position. Conversely, considering the socio-cultural dimensions of electoral support, moderately tightening up on cultural issues by means of assuming anti-immigrant stances has a positive impact on electoral performance, even in tandem with a high level of intra-party dissent. In both cases, electoral performance improves with a

---

[111] Although holding Euroskeptic attitudes positively influences the electoral support towards the Five Star Movement, we do not consider the policy dimension related to European issues at this stage of the analysis as we deem it is not influential in orienting the electoral support towards a political party at regional level.

tightening of the party's ideological positioning on both dimensions of electoral support.

Based on a spatial analysis of party competition (see Tables 5.2-5.4 below), this chapter investigates the ideological evolution of both M5S and its electoral competitors in relation to immigration-related issues and economic orientation toward redistributive policies. We also include the ideological positioning of parties on the traditional left/right dimension. The analysis demonstrates that M5S has tended to adopt an ambiguous stance on socio-cultural issues, especially compared to the consistent positions adopted by its right-wing electoral competitors. Indeed, the M5S has increasingly called for more restrictive migration containment measures over time, particularly starting from 2014. Conversely, as expected of populist radical right parties, the populist radical right League and Brothers of Italy parties adopted a static and near identical anti-immigrant stance on the immigration dimension.

However, M5S's moderate change in favor of implementing more restrictive measures to counter illegal immigration alongside high levels of intra-party dissent on the issue arguably reduced the chance for the party to increase its electoral performance at the regional level (i.e., elections) after 2018. Regarding the socioeconomic dimension of electoral support, the empirical analysis demonstrates how M5S's ideological positions on redistributive policies appear to be motivated by left-wing ideology rather than corresponding to a clear story about ambiguity. Nevertheless, M5S's increasing support for redistributive policies does not positively affect its overall electoral performance if accompanied by a high degree of intra-party dissent. This appears to confirm M5S's attempt to set the political agenda on different issues from the ones at the center of the radical right League's political campaign, such as immigration and internal security.

We highlight that during the first coalition government (i.e., Conte I Cabinet) between M5S and the League, the former launched the so-called Citizenship Income, a redistribution of wealth measure. On the other hand, this is consistent with recent studies on the Italian structure of the policy space (see Giannetti et al., 2018) highlighting the predominance of non-economic domains affecting party competition in the period of the 2018 Italian national parliamentary election, which made a government alliance possible between political parties with contradictory and vastly different positions from both a fiscal and welfare policy perspective (i.e., M5S and the League). Indeed, the ideological positioning of the government allies in 2019 is almost the opposite of the redistributive issue. Therefore, M5S appears as a deeply internally divided political party when it is not focused on an anti-system (i.e., populist) rhetoric.

The CHES expert survey data confirms the lack of internal cohesion of M5S in showing that, compared to all the other main political parties in Italy, M5S has the highest level of intra-party dissent on both the socioeconomic and cultural dimensions of electoral support. We argue that the lack of internal cohesion on immigration alongside redistributive issues, which are the specific attitudinal drivers that led voters to express their consensus toward the party, has conceivably prevented the electorate from fully understanding the primary reasons behind the change in M5S's ideological positioning on these key issues, in recent years.

Table 5.2 Main Political Parties in Italy & Issue Blurring

Political Party	Party Family	EU Integration: Blurry -2019	GALTAN: Blurry (2019)	Left-Right Economic Position: Blurry -2019
Five Star Movement (M5S)	Valence Populist	6.3	4.9	6.1
Lega (LN)	Radical Right	3.1	0.8	3.6
Fratelli d'Italia (FdI)	Radical Right	1.5	0.5	4.4
Democratic Party (PD)	Center-left	1.9	3.1	3.2
Forza Italia (FI)	Center Right	5	4	2.3
	CHES AVERAGE (2019)	3.4	2.9	3.6

Note: Figures rounded up or down to 1 decimal place. Source: CHES (2019)

Table 5.3 Main Political Parties in Italy and Issue Dissent

Political Party	Party Family	EU Dissent (2019 and 2017)	Immigration Dissent (2019 and 2017)	Left-Right Economic Position: Dissent (2019)
Five Star Movement (M5S)	Valence Populist	2019: 5.5	2019: 5.4	6.9
		2017: 4.1	2017: 4.8	
Lega (LN)	Radical Right	2019: 2.8	2019: 0.2	2.9
		2017: 1.2	2017: 0.1	
Fratelli d'Italia (FdI)	Radical Right	2019: 0.6	2019: 0.3	2.8
		2017: 0.3	2017: 0.8	
Democratic Party (PD)	Center-left	2019: 1.6	2019: 3.6	5.4
		2017: 3	2017: 4.1	
Forza Italia (FI)	Center Right	2019: 4.1	2019: 3.8	4
		2017: 4.8	2017: 3.1	
	CHES AVERAGE (2019)	2.6	2.7	2.9

Note: Figures rounded up or down to 1 decimal place. Source: CHES (2019 & 2017).

Table 5.4 Main Political Parties' Degree of Intraparty Dissent on a 10-point scale

Political Party	Social and Cultural Values	Ideological Stance on Economic Issues
Five Star Movement (M5S)	2019: 5.88	2019: 6.86
League (L)	2019: 1.00	2019: 2.86
Brothers of Italy (FdI)	2019: 0.88	2019: 2.57
Democratic Party (PD)	2019: 2.38	2019: 5.43
Forward Italy (FI)	2019: 4.50	2019: 4.00

Source: 2019 Chapel Hill Expert Survey Data.

Implications for the future of M5S: volatility

This chapter has aimed to expand the literature on the electoral fortunes of populist parties (particularly the case of unique populist parties, which are neither ideologically left nor right) (see de Jonge, 2020; Pauwels, 2011; De Lange and Art, 2011; Luther, 2011; Heinisch, 2003) in investigating the potential factors that have led unique valence populist parties such as M5S to experience a significant electoral decline. This chapter examined the electoral debacle of the unique populist M5S Party that occurred shortly after its resounding success at the 2018 Italian general election. We argue that the party's lack of intra-party unity and its tendency to adopt different and contradictory positions on several key issues that are meaningful for its electorate has led the party to experience a drastic reduction in its electoral performance.

The existing literature has examined the electoral decline and failures of populist radical right parties in recent years, spanning the Benelux countries (de Jonge, 2021), Belgium (de Jonge, 2020; Pauwels, 2011), the Netherlands (De Lange and Art, 2011) and Austria (Luther, 2011). Heinisch's (2003) seminal study investigated populist radical right parties' failure in government and drew on the case of the Freedom Party of Austria alongside populists.

This chapter focused on political parties' specific features to investigate M5S's electoral decline (i.e., at the party level) in regional elections that occurred after its government coalition agreement with the radical right League party in 2018. We argue that the main causes of M5S's electoral decline are multifaceted. In essence, M5S has self-sabotaged electorally due to its high degree of intra-party dissent alongside the party's tendency to change its positions on issues that are important for its electorate. More specifically, we argue that incredibly low levels of intra-party unity make it distinctly difficult for the party to maintain clear positions on the key issues that structure contemporary Italian politics. We also built on key comparative-level findings from the party politics literature, which highlight the negative effect of holding ambiguous party stances (see Lin and Lehrer, 2020; Plescia et al., 2020; Steiner and Mader, 2019; Somer-Topcu, 2015). In contrast, M5S's radical right electoral competitors, the League, and Brothers of Italy, have tended to adopt much clearer positions on a wide range of sociocultural issues, and this has likely enhanced the latter's electoral performance in recent years.

Although it is not unusual for political parties' leaders to attribute national significance to the results achieved in a regional election, even linking the fate of the government in power to the electoral victory or defeat that occurs at a regional level, we highlight the importance to reperform the empirical analysis relying on nationally based data (i.e., examining M5S's electoral performance after the 2022 Italian general election). However, we point out that our chapter makes an important contribution to the party politics literature. We find significant patterns relating directly to the electoral decline of M5S and the rise of radical right challenger parties (Lega and FdI) in contemporary Italian party politics within the wider context of electoral volatility in contemporary Italian politics (see Pirro, 2018; Zulianello, 2020).

Conclusion

The main argument in this chapter is that M5S's post-2018 Italian general election decline is multifaceted, with key explanations including the party's ideological ambiguity on a wide range of issues and high levels of intra-party dissent. We have also identified a paradox in this chapter concerning M5S's overall electoral fortunes as a populist party in contemporary Italian politics. What initially led to M5S's astonishing electoral rise at the 2018 Italian general election (unique key features such as a loose party organization/internal party structure, ambiguity on policy issues, grassroots activism, and direct democracy) has now arguably become an electoral hindrance (i.e., an Achilles's heel) for the party.

Fast forward two years from the 2018 national parliamentary election, and what is even more astonishing is M5S's systematic electoral decline. Recent regional election results and public opinion polls show a party in chaos through various ideological and intra-party disputes, alongside the party crisscrossing blurred lines between being both a populist and an establishment party (i.e., featuring in the last three coalition governments post-2018). The M5S Party continued its sharp electoral decline at the most recent 2022 national parliamentary election, losing a staggering 175 seats in the Chamber of Deputies and 84 seats in the Senate. M5S now finds itself out of power (government), with Prime Minister Giorgia Meloni heading up a radical right coalition that features FdI, the League, alongside FI.

This chapter built on three main areas of literature that comprise (a) populism in Italian politics by means of further investigating the ideologically ambiguous nature of M5S (see Zulianello, 2020) alongside the party's fluctuating electoral fortunes and (b) the comparative party politics literature (see Lin and Lehrer, 2020 and Somer-Topcu, 2015) in outlining how intra-party features such as the degree of intra-party dissent and the change in the ideological positioning on key policy positions have impacted negatively on M5S's overall support. (c) The chapter has also built on the wider populism literature that deals with the electoral decline of populist parties (particularly populist radical right parties) (see de Jonge, 2020; Pauwels, 2011; De Lange and Art, 2011; Luther, 2011; Heinisch, 2003).

The chapter provided a comprehensive analysis of the different factors that have contributed to the recent electoral decline of the populist M5S Party in Italian politics. Therefore, our findings constitute a preliminary attempt to systematically study the electoral decline of the unique valence populist M5S Party within the exceptional case of Italian politics, thereby linking parties' electoral fortunes to parties' specific features and the perception of their levels of clarity/ambiguity alongside cohesion/dissent.

Although the M5S Party has been in three successive coalition governments, its ideological future looks increasingly uncertain, especially in the context of the current economic situation in Italy and the party's poor showing at the 2022 Italian national parliamentary election. Therefore, the main argument in this chapter is that M5S's capacity to adopt ideologically ambiguous stances, especially concerning socio-cultural issues, alongside its internal dissent and heterogeneity, has harmed the party electorally.

References

Albertazzi, D., and Vampa, D. (Eds.) (2021). *Populism and New Patterns of Political Competition in Western Europe*. Extremism & Democracy Series. London: Routledge.

Bakker, R., Hooghe, L., Jolly, S., Marks, G., Polk, J., Rovny, J., Steenbergen, M., and Vachudova, M.A. (2020). 2019 Chapel Hill Expert Survey. Version 2019.1. Available on chesdata.eu. Chapel Hill, NC: University of North Carolina, Chapel Hill.

Bélanger, É., and Meguid, B.M., (2008). Issue salience, issue ownership and issue-based vote choice. *Electoral Studies*, 27 (3): 477–491.

Benoit, K., and Laver, M. (2006). *Party Policy in Modern Democracies*. London: Routledge.

Budge, I. (1982). Strategies, Issues, and Votes: British General Elections, 1950-1979. *Comparative Political Studies*, 15(2):171-196.

Conti, N. (2014). New Parties and the Transformation of the Italian Political Space. *Contemporary Italian Politics*, 6(3): 205-221.

Conti, N., and Memoli, V. (2015). The Emergence of a New Party in the Italian Party System: Rise and Fortunes of the Five Star Movement. *West European Politics*, 38:3: 516-534.

Corbetta, P., and Gualmini, E. (2013). *Il partito di Grillo*. Bologna: il Mulino.

de Jonge, L. (2020). The curious case of Belgium: Why is there no right-wing populism in Wallonia? *Government and Opposition*: 1-17.

de Jonge, L. (2021). *The Success and Failure of Right-Wing Populist Parties in the Benelux Countries*. London: Routledge.

De Lange, S. L., and Art, D. (2011). Fortuyn versus Wilders: An agency-based approach to radical right party building. *West European Politics*, 34(6): 1229-1249.

Di Virgilio, A., Giannetti, D. and Pedrazzani, A. (2014). Party Competition in the 2013 Italian Elections: Evidence from an Expert Survey. *Government and Opposition*, 50(1): 65–89.

Dolezal, M., Ennser-Jedenastik, L., Müller, W.C., Winkler, A.K. (2014). How Parties Compete for Votes: a Test of Saliency Theory. *European Journal of Political Research*, 53(1): 57-76.

Downes, J.F., Loveless, M. and Lam, A. (2021). The Looming Refugee Crisis in the EU: Right-Wing Party Competition and Strategic Positioning. *JCMS: Journal of Common Market Studies*.

Downes, J.F., and Loveless, M. (2018). Center Right and Radical Right Party Competition in Europe: Strategic Emphasis on Immigration, Anti-Incumbency, and Economic Crisis. *Electoral Studies*, 54: 148-158.

Downs, A. (1957). *An Economic Theory of Democracy*. New York: Harper and Row. ed P. Corbetta and E. Gualmini, Il Mulino: 89–122.

Franzosi, P., Marone, F. and Salvati, E. (2015). Populism and Euroskepticism in the Italian Five Star Movement, *The International Spectator*, 50(2): 109-124.

Giannetti, D., Pedreazzani, A. and Pinto, L. (2016). Party System Change in Italy: Politicising the EU and the Rise of Eccentric Parties. *South European Society and Politics*, 22(1): 21-42.

Giannetti, D., Pedrazzani, A. and Pinto, L. (2018). The rising importance of Non-Economic Policy Dimensions and the Formation of the Conte Government in Italy. *Italian Political Science*, 13(2): 27-44.

Hawkins, K.A., Carlin, R.E., Littvay, L., and Rovira Kaltwasser, C. (2019). *The Ideational Approach to Populism: Concept, Theory and Analysis*. Abingdon: Routledge.

Heinisch, R. (2003). Success in opposition–failure in government: explaining the performance of right-wing populist parties in public office. *West European Politics*, 26(3): 91-130.

Hinich, M.J. and Munger, M.C. (1992). A Spatial Theory of Ideology. *Journal of Theoretical*

Lin, N. and Lehrer R. (2020). Everything to Everyone and the Conditioning Effect of Intraparty Cohesion: a Replication in a Cross-National Context. *Party Politics 27* (5), 909–916.

Luther, K. R. (2011). Of goals and own goals: A case study of right-wing populist party strategy for and during incumbency. *Party Politics*, 17(4): 453-470.

Manucci, L., and Amsler, M. (2018). Where the wind blows: Five Star Movement's populism, direct democracy and ideological flexibility. *Italian Political Science Review*, 48(1): 109-132.

Mudde, C. (2004). The Populist Zeitgeist. *Government and Opposition*, 39 (3): 541–563.

Mudde, C. (2007). *Populist Radical Right Parties in Europe*. Cambridge: Cambridge University Press.

Mudde, C. (2014). The far-right and the European elections. *Current History*, 113 (761): 98-103.

Pauwels, T. (2021). Explaining the strange decline of the populist radical right Vlaams Belang in Belgium: The impact of permanent opposition. *Acta Politica, 46(1): 60-82*.

Pedrazzani, A. and Pinto, L. (2013). Gli Elettori del Movimento 5 Stelle, in Il partito di Grillo,

Pedrazzani, A. and Pinto, L. (2015). The Electoral Base: the 'Political Revolution' in Evolution'. In F. Tronconi (Ed.) *Beppe Grillo's Five Star Movement. Organisation, Communication and Ideology.* (pp. 75-98). London: Ashgate.

Pirro, A. L. P., and P. Taggart. (2018). The Populist Politics of Euroskepticism in Times of Crisis: A Framework for Analysis. *Politics*, 38(3): 253-262.

Pirro, A. L. P. (2018). The Polyvalent Populism of the 5 Star Movement. *Journal of Contemporary European Studies*, 26(4): 443-458.

Plescia, C., Kritzinger, S. and Eberl, J-M. (2020). 'The Enemy within': Campaign Attention and Motivated Reasoning in Voter Perceptions of Intra-Party Conflict. *Party Politics*. 4(1): 5-30.

Polk, J., Rovny, J., Bakker, R., Edwards, E., Hooghe, L., Jolly, S., Koedam, J., Kostelka, F., Marks, G., Schumacher, G., Steenbergen, M., Vachudova, M.A., and Zilovic, M. (2017). Explaining the Salience of Anti-Elitism and Reducing Political Corruption for Political Parties in Europe with the 2014 Chapel Hill Expert Survey Data. *Research & Politics*, (January-March): 1-9.

Rovny, J. (2012). Who Emphasizes and Who Blurs? Party Strategies in Multidimensional *Competition. European Union Politics*, 13(2): 269-292.

Russo, L., Riera, P, and Verthé, T. (2017). Tracing the electorate of the Movimento Cinque Stelle: an ecological inference analysis. *Italian Political Science Review*, 47(1): 45-62.

Somer-Topcu, Z. (2015). Everything to Everyone: the Electoral Consequences of the Broad-Appeal Strategy in Europe. *American Journal of Political Science*, 59(4): 841-854.

Steiner, N.D.N. and Mader, M. (2019). Intra-Party Heterogeneity in Policy Preferences and its Effect on Issue Salience: Developing and Applying a Measure Based on Elite Survey Data. *Party Politics*, 25(3): 336-348.

Taggart, P. (2000). *Populism. Buckingham*: London: Open University Press.

Van Kessel, S. (2015*). Populist parties in Europe: Agents of discontent?* New York: Springer.

Zulianello, M. (2020). Varieties of Populist Parties and Party Systems in Europe: From State-of-the-Art to the Application of a Novel Classification Scheme to 66 Parties in 33 Countries. *Government and Opposition*: 55(2), 327-347.

PART THREE
The Future of the Italian Radical Right

Chapter 6
The Italian Center-right Coalition and Transnational Cleavage

The political and economic consequences of World War II aroused an urgent need in the minds of the Italian political elites to demand a stronger alliance of European countries at the transnational level in order to avoid any further military conflict within the old continent. Italy has always been at the forefront of the European integration process for several reasons. First, Italy wanted to be considered equal with the other (victorious) European countries of World War II; second, the Italian government wanted to increase its diplomatic ties with the US (which invested massively in European reconstruction against the Soviet threat); and, third, the Italian people are still reeling from the totalitarian fascist experience[112]. European integration offers an opportunity for Italy to initiate a new democratic process (Varsori, 2010). Therefore, the Italian governments of the 1950s played a leading role in the building of a new transnational community. Ultimately, driven by a strong desire for reconstruction and friendship among European people, Belgium, France, Italy, the Federal Republic of Germany, Luxembourg, and the Netherlands jointly signed the Treaty of Paris in 1951 (establishing the European Coal and Steel Community—ECSC) and the Treaties of Rome in 1957 (establishing the European Economic Community—EEC),

---

[112] We should not forget that Italy is a country weakened by the war militarily, politically, and economically. Furthermore, although a substantial part of the Italian people joined the resistance movement, the Italian electorate of the 1950s had not yet accepted democratic values. Indeed, looking at the Italian political landscape of the time, there are parties, both on the left (the Italian Communist Party) and on the right (the National Monarchist Party and the Italian Social Movement), that openly declared themselves as revolutionary and/or anti-system movements, reaching a total of 30–35% of support in the Italian electorate. For this reason, the pro-European choice of the Italian governments (largely controlled by the Christian Democratic party) is primarily driven by the goal of improving the country's economy and embracing the values of democratic regimes tying with a double knot Italy with the other European democratic powers (Varsori, 2010).

which were the first bricks that composed the foundations of the EU.

Subsequently, in the 1960s and 1970s, the Italian political elite became polarized with regard to the European integration process. On the one hand, the Italian Communist Party (PCI) forcefully opposed subsequent steps of the European integration process because of their skepticism toward the Common Market as adverse to the Italian economic system and a threat to the European continent to achieve peace since the European integration process was perceived as a 'provocation' to the Soviet Union (Mueller, 2010). On the other hand, the Italian Christian Democracy (DC) sustained the EEC as a chance for Italy to play a leading role at the international level and, again, to consolidate the Italian alliance with the US. Nevertheless, over the years, left-wing parties, including PCI, gradually changed their position toward the EEC, resulting in a reduced polarization of the Italian party system with regard to the European integration process (Conti and Verzichelli, 2005).

Afterward, from the early 1980s to the early 1990s, the Italian political elite was able to sustain policies in pursuit of more economic and political unification of the EEC countries without suffering from political blame in implementing significant institutional reforms and delegating national authority to transnational institutions, such as the signing of the Single European Act (SEA) aiming for the completion of the Single Market and the aggrandizement of Southern Europe including Greece, Spain and Portugal. The literature on European politics defines this period as the "permissive consensus" (Daniels, 1998: 107), where Italy was "long regarded as the most pro-European of the continent" both at the country and party levels (Serricchio, 2012: 115).

However, since the signing of the Maastricht Treaty in 1992, the ideological conflict between pro-EU vs. anti-EU has played a significant role in all the European member states' party systems, including the Italian one (Hooghe and Marks, 2018). For that reason, we aim to explore to what extent the transnational cleavage developed within the Italian party system since the beginning of the Second Republic, which coincided with the signing of the Maastricht Treaty and then focus on to what extent the parties constituting the Italian center-right coalition have addressed this new ideological conflict recently.

With this goal in mind, since the early 2000s, as "a true cottage industry" (Mudde, 2012: 193), a great number of scholars have increased in describing the phenomenon of Euroskepticism, relying on different theoretical approaches. In this chapter, we mostly rely on studies produced by the 'North Carolina School' which analyzes how party politics address the conflict between pro-EU vs. anti-EU, identifying it as a new ideological conflict (or cleavage structure) that impacts current European party systems and political debates, including Italy. To this end, this chapter will first review the more recent literature that attempts to conceptualize the notion of Euroskepticism, and it will also re-examine the new transnational cleavage conceptualized by Hooghe and Marks (2018), proposing an innovative *multidimensional* approach to this new ideological conflict. Second, relying on data from the Eurobarometer (EB) and the Comparative Manifesto Project (CMP), we will show how the new transnational cleavage is operationalized in practice in order to depict both factors of the demand side and supply side of political parties. In the third part, we will present results first to verify whether (and to what extent) Italy has been polarized both at the country (demand side) and party level (supply side) since the beginning of the Second Republic (from 1994 to 2018). Then, the analysis of the new transnational cleavage is deepened, focusing on the center-right wing coalition (League, Brothers of Italy and Forward Italy).

The new transnational cleavage: an ideological conflict more complex than we previously thought

Euroskepticism, a complex and debated concept in European politics has proven to be a challenging subject for scholars. Although a considerable amount of literature exists on this topic, there is little consensus and much disagreement regarding its key components (Szczerbiak and Taggart, 2008). One area where scholars do find agreement is the origin of Euroskepticism. While earlier academic work viewed Euroskepticism primarily as an extension of nationalism, the post-Maastricht era shifted the focus toward the European integration process itself as the historical juncture responsible for generating this ideological conflict (Crespy and Verschueren, 2009). However, the very meaning of Euroskepticism remains a topic of debate due to its ambiguous nature (Leruth et al., 2018). Despite its unclear definition from the British mass media, the term found its way into academic literature and was employed to describe any form of opposition to the EU (Spiering, 2004). After a series of attempts to explore the very nature of Euroskepticism (see, e.g., Szczerbiak and Taggart, 2008), we argue that Hooghe and Marks (2018) offer the most comprehensive definition of Euroskepticism by incorporating it into the framework of cleavage theory (Lipset and Rokkna, 1967). They conceptualize Euroskepticism as a political ideology in opposition to Europeanism. This division has become a central element in European party competition, pitting pro-EU against anti-EU forces (see also Marks et al., 2002; Kriesi and Grande, 2015). Nevertheless, Hooghe and Marks' framework, although effective, does not capture the full spectrum of nuances within Europeanism and Euroskepticism. We believe that transnational cleavage can be understood as a multidimensional conflict, with various dimensions generating their own ideological pull. This view aligns with the idea of multidimensionality in complex political issues proposed by Baumgartner and Jones (2002) and Gattinara (2016). Accordingly, we identify three dimensions of conflict within transnational cleavage: an institutional dimension (Lindberg and Scheingold, 1970; Feld and Wildgen, 1976; Handley, 1981; Eichenberg and Dalton, 2007), an economic dimension (Tsebelis and Garrett, 2000; Leupold, 2015) and a cultural dimension (Taggart, 1998; McLaren, 2002). Each dimension presents antithetical positions, including 'European Federalism vs. National Souverainisme', 'Marketism vs. Protectionism', and 'Multiculturalism vs. Nativism'. This reconceptualization of transnational cleavage is thus in line with the North Carolina school idea of the EU being so socially rooted within current European societies that it reinforces a new dimension of conflict that challenges pre-existing classical cleavages such as Left vs. Right. Additionally, it provides the advantage of exploring whether individuals and political parties can adopt stances that allow them to employ elements from both Euroskepticism and Europeanism. Drawing from this new reconceptualization, in the following section, we will explain how to operationalize in practice in order to depict the new transnational cleavage at both the individual level (demand side) and party level (supply side).

Operationalizing the new transnational cleavage structure

The main data source to explore the transnational cleavage at the individual level is the standard version of the EB, which has been published twice a year (spring and autumn) since 1973. We selected this data[113] source because it is particularly well suited to analyze trends of public opinion with variables that can represent each dimension of transnational cleavage.

Starting with the institutional dimension, we will employ the 'membership good/bad'[114] question. This variable has already been used to explore support/opposition to the European integration project from an institutional perspective (Lindberg and Scheingold, 1970; Feld and Wildgen, 1976; Handley, 1981). In fact, this trend question best depicts such dimension since "membership in the EU represents the existential fact of the integration process – endorsing membership is therefore endorsing the process of integration itself" (Eichenberg and Dalton, 2007: 133). Moving to the economic

---

[113] In order to explore data from the early 1990s to the late 2010s, we integrated the following EBs: EB42, EB43.1, EB44.1, EB46, EB47.1, EB49, EB50, EB52, EB53, EB54.1, EB56.2, EB57.1, EB58.1, EB59.1, EB60.1, EB61, EB62, EB64.2, EB73.4, EB91.5.

[114] The question is formulated as follows: "Generally speaking, do you think that (your country's) membership of the European Community (common market) is [...]? (1) A good thing, (2) neither good nor bad, (3) a bad thing" (excluding the DK and NA categories). By merging the last two categories, we can observe, on the one hand, all those respondents that are clearly in support of the EU membership, and on the other hand, those that are not totally convinced of the EU integration project. I, therefore, relabelled these categories as 0 for 'European federalism' and as 1 for 'national souverainisme'.

dimension, we selected the "membership country benefit"[115] question to capture respondents' attitudes with regard to the economic calculations between the costs and benefits of being part of the EU (McLaren, 2002: 522). With regards to the last dimension of transnational cleavage, the cultural dimension is represented by the 'National vs. European identity'[116] question. This variable was already employed to explore the extent to which European integration might be hindered not only for institutional or economic reasons but also because of concerns about the dissolution of national identity (McLaren, 2002: 554). Finally, moving to transnational cleavage (as a whole), this ideological conflict was constructed by combining the three variables that we just described above. To accomplish this, an individual will be defined as anti-EU when they hold at least two negative stands out of three toward the EU, and they will be defined as pro-EU when they hold at least two positive stands out of three toward the EU (see a similar work from Emanuele et al., 2020: 320).

Moving to the operationalization of transnational cleavage at the party level, the main data source is the CMP dataset (Werner et al., 2011). This data source is one of the most used in comparative politics to explore the supply side of political parties. In fact, the CMP team provides an invaluable amount of data, manually coding electoral manifestos of political parties from over 50 countries since the end of World War II. The electoral manifestos are coded in units of analysis named quasi-sentences. Each unit represents only one message (thus only one category). To explore the

---

[115] The question is "Taking everything into consideration, would you say that (your country) has on balance benefited or not from being a member of the European community (common Market)? (1) Benefited, (2) Not Benefited" (excluding the DK and NA categories). Eventually, we respectively relabelled these categories as 0 for 'marketism' and as 1 for 'protectionism'.

[116] The question is structured as follows; "In the near future do you see yourself as? (1) <nationality> only, (2) <nationality> and European, (3) European and <nationality> and (4) European only" (excluding the DK and NA categories). Therefore, in order to represent the dichotomist nature of this dimension I have recoded the variables as follows: 0 for '<nationality> and European', 'European and <nationality>' and 'European only' and as 1 for '<nationality> only'. In this way, I relabelled these two categories as 0 for 'multiculturalism' and as 1 for 'nativism'.

development of transnational cleavage at the party level in Italy, we employ these data because CMP also provides categories that best represent all dimensions of transnational cleavage.

Starting with the institutional dimension, this is associated with the categories (108) European Community/Integration: Positive and (110) European Community/Integration: Negative. These categories respectively coincide with the dichotomy 'European Federalism' and the dichotomy 'National Souverainisme'. The economic dimension is constructed, on the one hand, by the CMP categories (401) Free Market Economy and (407) Protectionism: Negative. Both categories favorably mention the free movement of goods and capital, defending processes at the basis of the liberal economic market. Thus, they jointly represent the dichotomy 'Marketism'. On the other hand, the CMP categories such as (403) Market Regulation, (406) Protectionism: Positive, (409) Keynesian Demand Management and (413) Nationalisation, favorably mention stances on government ownership of industries, economic stimulus by the government in periods of economic crisis (against austerity) and the extension of protectionist measures to disincentivize the movement of capital and goods across countries. These categories constitute the dichotomy 'Protectionism'.

The cultural dimension is associated with CMP categories (602) National Way of Life: Negative and (607) Multiculturalism: Positive, which represents favorable mentions toward cultural diversity, immigration and opposition to nationalism. Instead, CMP categories (601) National Way of Life: Positive and (608) Multiculturalism: Negative are stances appealing to nationalism, patriotism and antagonization with cultural diversity or immigration. The first pair of categories coincide with the dichotomy 'Multiculturalism', and the second pair of categories coincide with the dichotomy 'Nativism'. To conclude, the transnational cleavage is constituted by all CMP categories presented above. Accordingly, the dichotomy 'Pro-EU' is measured through all categories linked to the dichotomies 'European Federalism', 'Marketism' and 'Multiculturalism', while the dichotomy 'Anti-EU' is measured with all categories linked to the dichotomies 'National Souverainisme', 'Protectionism' and 'Nativism'.

The CMP team suggests three main techniques to conceptually depict the supply side of political parties (Laver and Budge, 1992): strategy, emphasis and position. In this study, we mostly rely on strategy as it shows both emphasis and position. In fact, parties' strategies are measured as the sum of all categories representing one dichotomy minus the sum of all categories representing the second dichotomy. Therefore, the resulting score ranges from –100 to +100 (strategy = dichotomy1–dichotomy2). Such party strategy is employed to depict whether and to what extent the center-left and center-right propose themselves as political alternatives on the new transnational cleavage. The parties' emphasis and position will be used to deepen the analysis of the parties constituting the center-right wing coalition.

The development of the new transnational cleavage structure in Italy

Following the widely acknowledged literature from above, we will now explore how transnational cleavage has changed in Italy. This section is divided into two parts. In the first one, drawing from previous scholars' recommendations (Rydgren 2007; Mudde 2007), we will explore how transnational cleavage has become a polarizing conflict at both the individual level (demand side) and party level (supply side). In the second part, we shall focus exclusively on the parties composing the center-right coalition to reveal similarities and differences among them with regard to the new transnational cleavage.

The metamorphosis of the Italian party system in the Second Republic

As stated above, this section depicts how individuals and political parties align with regard to the new transnational cleavage in Italy from 1994 to 2018. Starting the analysis at the individual level, Figure 6.1 shows how the new transnational cleavage has developed since the beginning of the Second Republic (until 2019). These results confirm that Italian public opinion is experiencing new processes of dealignment that increase the level of polarization with regard to the new transnational cleavage. Overall, Figure 6.1 shows three main stages of change within Italian public opinion. From 1994 to 2002, most Italians held pro-EU attitudes with regard to transnational cleavage in a range between 78% and 84%. Then, from 2002 to 2005, there is a first decrease in pro-EU consent from 78% to 61%. Finally, the new transnational cleavage has deepened so much within Italian society since 2005 that, for the very first time, Italians are perfectly polarized (50%:50%) on this new ideological conflict in 2019.

Figure 6.1 Dealignments of the new transnational cleavage at the individual level from 1994 to 2018

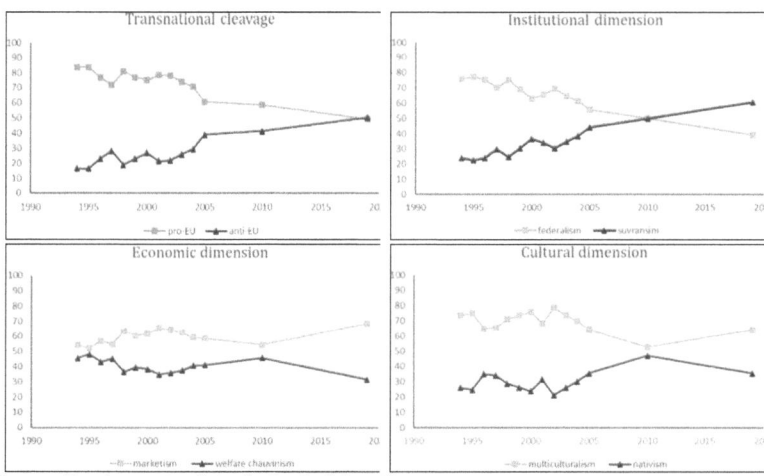

Source: Eurobarometer data. Author's elaboration.

The reasons behind this new dealignment within Italian public opinion can be observed in Figure 6.1 when focusing on each dimension composing the new transnational cleavage. In fact, we can observe that from 1994 to 2002, all dimensions show that the majority of Italians hold positive attitudes toward the EU (European federalism, marketism and multiculturalism). Moreover, it should be noted that among the three dimensions, the economic dimension is the one that was more polarized in 1994, but the marketism attitude tended to increase in the following years until 2001, reaching its peak at 65%. Therefore, these results demonstrate that public opinion did not react against the EU in the following years after the signing of the Maastricht Treaty. By contrast, most Italians held positive attitudes toward the EU at this first stage (institutional and cultural dimensions) and even the number of people who believe in the economic beneficial effects of the European membership has increased.

However, although Italians did not greet the Maastricht Treaty with skepticism, subsequent events linked to the European integration process made the EU more visible in the eyes of Italian citizens, who started to recognize the extent to which the European institutions can impact their daily lifestyles and, eventually, increased the level of skepticism toward the EU. For instance, in the period from 2002 to 2005, we can observe the first substantial decrease in Italians that favored the EU in all three dimensions of the new transnational cleavage. The literature often explains the spur of dissent against the EU because of the European enlargement process toward Eastern European countries in 2004. In fact, this enlargement was perceived by the Italian public as a threat both from an economic and a cultural point of view. Economically speaking, the inclusion of poorer regions of Eastern Europe meant an impact on the structural redistribution of the EU budget, which mostly favored the Mediterranean regions (including regions from Southern Italy) (Serricchio, 2012). Culturally speaking, from the heritage of the Cold War conflict between East vs. West, Western populations (including Italians) did not consider the people from Eastern Europe as truly Europeans, deepening a cultural clash between 'old' vs. 'new' European people (Schimmelfennig and Sedelmeier, 2002).

Finally, from 2005 to 2019, Figure 6.1 shows that the Italian public opinion is perfectly polarized with regard to the new transnational cleavage (as a whole). Nevertheless, when focusing on the dimensions of this new conflict, we can observe that the institutional dimension is the one that is playing a significant role in decreasing the number of people in favor of the EU. The reason behind this phenomenon is because of two major crises that have worsened the Italians' view on the usefulness of the EU in handling transnational issues: the Eurozone crisis in 2010 and the migration crisis in 2015 (Scipioni, 2018; Anderson, 2021). With regards to the Eurozone crisis, according to Bellucci (2014: 248), most Italians criticized the EU austerity plan, which was delivered at the time by Prime Minister Mario Monti (a former European commissioner).

While linked to the migration crisis, the normative consequences of the Dublin Treaty, which dropped the responsibility to the peripheral countries to host refugees, have driven Italians to mostly blame the EU for abandoning Italy in the management of the migration crisis (Barbulescu and Beaudonnet, 2014; Conti et al., 2020).

Over the decades, these data demonstrate that Italians do not approve or oppose the EU outright, but they rather differently support and oppose some dimensions constituting the new transnational cleavage. In fact, the picture that we can draw from Figure 6.1 is that Italians used to endorse the European integration process in the 1980s completely. While in the most recent years (2019), most Italians still consider European membership as a benefit for their national economy, and they also tend to consider themselves more Europeans than Italians. Nevertheless, results from Figure 6.1 also demonstrate that Italians are mostly skeptical of the EU with regard to the institutional dimension, which undermines the ideological basis of the EU foundation to raise the European countries on the world stage as key players.

Now, shifting the focus at the party level, we will explore how the Italian coalition governments (center-left and center-right) have addressed the new transnational cleavage in the last seven political campaigns during the Italian general elections (from 1994 to 2018). First, we can see from Figure 6.2 that the new transnational cleavage does not occupy a significant space in political parties' manifestos. Indeed, we can see that both coalitions never dedicate more than 5% of their manifestos to this topic (except for the center-right coalition in 2008). However, in terms of dealignment between coalitions, we can observe two main periods that demonstrate that the new transnational cleavage became, from election to election, a more polarizing topic at the party level. For instance, from 1994 to 2006, the center-right and the center-left coalitions do not experience a considerable level of dealignment on the new transnational cleavage. They do not attempt to present themselves to the Italian electorate as two alternative political offers, but they are rather similar in both terms of emphasis (low) and position (pro-EU). However, from 2008 to 2018, the two coalitions start to address the new transnational cleavage differently. On the one hand, the center-left

174   THE RISE OF THE RADICAL RIGHT IN ITALY

coalition steadily shifts from a neutral to a pro-EU strategy (most notably in 2018). On the other hand, the center-right coalition fluctuated more than the center-left coalition as it moved from a strong opposition against the EU in 2008 to a moderately negative strategy in 2013, and finally, it returned to an anti-EU strategy in 2018. These results confirm our expectations that, like the individual level, there was no dealignment between the two coalitions in the subsequent years after the signing of the Maastricht Treaty, but they eventually started to offer two political alternatives to their electorates on the European issue from the late 2010s onwards.

Figure 6.2   Alignments of the new transnational cleavage at the party level from 1994 to 2018

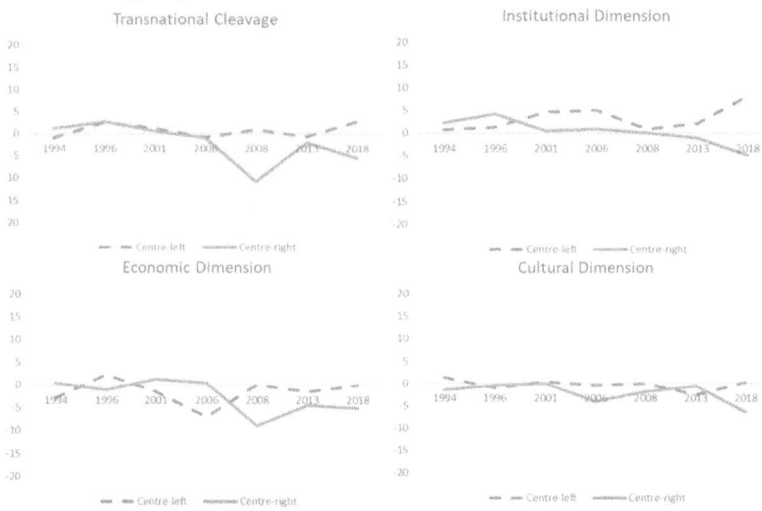

Source: CMP data. Author's elaboration.

We shall focus now on each dimension to explore which dimension impacted this new dealignment process at the party level on the European issue. In fact, at first sight, we can observe that the center-left and the center-right coalitions experienced each dimension of the new transnational cleavage over the years differently. Starting with the institutional dimension, the center-left coalition shows to have always supported the EU. It usually holds a neutral strategy, but it also demonstrated institutional support of the European integration process, especially in the years of the great left-wing coalitions (composed of both left-wing and radical left-wing parties) in 2001 and 2006 and, more recently, in 2018.

This increase of Europeanism at the institutional dimension within the center-left coalition coincided with the presidency at the EC of Romano Prodi from 1999 to 2004. Romano Prodi is one of the founders of the left-wing coalition, and his presidency at the EC was characterized by some of the most important events that advanced the European integration process (e.g., the introduction of the Euro currency and expansion to the East). By contrast, the center-right coalition gradually changed its strategy on this dimension, shifting from a federalist strategy in the 1990s to a neutral strategy in the 2000s and finally standing for the dichotomy 'souverainism' in the 2010s. Kertzer (2015), for instance, considers Romani Prodi's EC presidency as the real root of this antagonization against the EU from the center-right coalition because Prodi is one of the founding leaders of the Italian left-wing and a long-time opponent of Silvio Berlusconi (leader of the center-right coalition).

However, it is within the economic dimension that the center-right coalition demonstrated most of its antagonization against the EU. In fact, the center-right coalition moved from a neutral strategy (from 1994 to 2006) into standing for the dichotomy 'Protectionism' since 2008. This shift of the center-right coalition is described by Quaglia (2008: 64) as the attempt to identify in the EU and, most importantly, the "lefts in Europe to be blamed for the poor economic performance" in Italy. In fact, throughout the 2001–2006 Berlusconi government, the center-right coalition developed a new narrative against the EU that overlapped with the more traditional conflict against the Italian center-left coalition. In this period, "numerous attacks on the EU and the Euro were made often by the Berlusconi allies" in blaming "Prodi and Brussels for placing Italy in this situation and for agreeing on Italy's entrance into the Eurozone at too high an exchange rate" (Brunazzo and Mascitelli, 2020). By contrast, except for one year (2006), the center-left coalition never exposed itself to the economic dimension, but it rather preferred keeping a neutral strategy during the entire period observed.

Finally, on the cultural dimension, we can observe that both coalitions did not considerably change in the last seven general elections. They both hold a neutral strategy with regard to the cultural dimension, although the center-right coalition slightly distinguished itself from the center-left coalition standing toward the dichotomy 'nativism', especially in 2018. To that end, during the 2018 general election, the center-right coalition strongly focused its electoral campaign on defending Italy from the uncontrolled migratory flows from Northern Africa and the Middle East (Geddes and Pettrachin, 2020).

Similar to the previous analysis, the multidimensional investigation of the new transnational cleavage offers the opportunity to reveal where political forces alternatively propose themselves to the Italian electorate. Thus, Figure 6.2 reveals that, since 2008, the center-left coalition has been neutral in all three dimensions, except for the institutional dimension in 2018. This result demonstrates that the Italian center-left coalition is not skeptical with regards to the EU, not even Euro-enthusiastic, except for its institutional dimension showing that the center-left coalition is keen to encourage a further *political* integration process at the transnational level. In contrast, in the same period, the center-right coalition has also been neutral toward the EU, except for the economic dimension. Eventually, in 2018, the center-right coalition drastically shifted its strategy against the EU in all its dimensions, revealing that the Italian center-right coalition has completely internalized the dichotomy 'anti-EU' in *all* its logics of conflict (dimensions).

Having demonstrated that the new transnational cleavage has become a polarizing topic both at the country and party levels, these results also reveal that the center-right coalition has drastically changed its strategy from pro-EU to anti-EU. The next section will show which right-wing party (or parties) have most influenced the political offer of the center-right coalition.

Alignments and dealignments within the center-right coalition on the new transnational cleavage

The analysis now turns to the center-right coalition. More specifically, we are interested in exploring the tripolar political alliance among the League, Brothers of Italy and Forward Italy. This coalition was originally founded in December 2012 in view of the 2013 general elections. Subsequently, it also proposed itself at the 2018 general elections. For that reason, we will examine elements of alignment and dealignment within the center-right on the new transnational cleavage from 2013 to 2018.

Figure 6.3, below, shows data on the emphasis and position employed by the three right-wing parties on the new transnational cleavage (and its dimensions) during the electoral campaigns. To begin with, the figure shows that the transnational cleavage (as a whole) reveals both elements of alignment and dealignment among the right-wing parties. Although all three parties increase their level of emphasis on the European issue and they tend to align toward the dichotomy 'souverainism', which supports the idea that transnational cleavage is particularly appealing for the right-wing and radical-right-wing parties; the results are not completely homogeneous across political parties in terms of position. Indeed, one can observe that the League and Brothers of Italy are particularly polarized on the dichotomy of 'souverainism'.

However, Forward Italy does not follow this pattern, but it rather stands in between a neutral and a moderate position toward the same dichotomy. To this extent, one can notice that the center-right coalition has changed from one election to another. In 2013, there would have been more similarities between the League and Forward Italy both in terms of emphasis (relatively moderate at 11%) and position (weakly pro-EU). In 2018, the League and Brothers of Italy proposed an opposite pattern, dedicating much more space to this new ideological conflict (respectively 18% and 22%) in their manifestos and holding a clear position (strongly anti-EU).

Figure 6.3 Alignments and dealignments within the centre-right coalition from 2013 to 2018

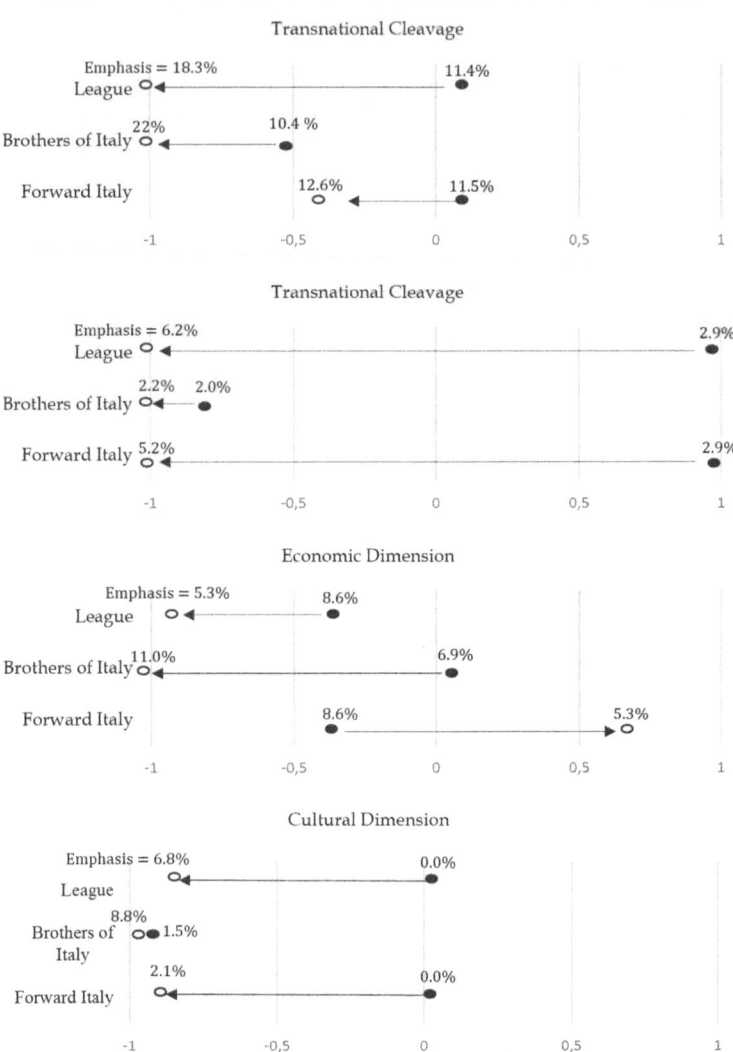

Source: CMP data. Author's elaboration

In a similar manner to the previous section, we now focus on framing strategies of the right-wing parties, looking at similarities and differences that can be traced among them in each dimension of the new transnational cleavage. Starting with the institutional dimension, we can observe phenomena of alignment and dealignment among the three right-wing parties from 2013 to 2018. On the one hand, we can observe that the parties align in terms of position standing for the dichotomy 'souverainism'. In fact, although the League and Forward Italy used to favor a more European integration process by jointly proposing "the direct popular election of the President of the EC" (PDL, 2013), they now consider the EU as "a gigantic supranational body, devoid of true democratic legitimacy" (League, 2018). For that reason, they demand a "revision of the European treaties" (Forward Italy, 2018) to restore national sovereignty. By contrast, Brothers of Italy remained more programmatically coherent from one election to another, describing the EU as "a bureaucratic and oligarchic Europe that often favors interests far from the common good" (Brothers of Italy, 2013) and, for that reason, it recently demanded "supremacy clause in the [Italian] Constitution to block [European] agreements and directives harmful to Italy" (Brothers of Italy). On the other hand, we can observe that there is some extent of dealignment among these parties in terms of emphasis. The institutional dimension of the transnational cleavage became of greater importance for the League and Forward Italy, which (almost) doubled the amount of space dedicated to this dimension from 2013 to 2018, while Brothers of Italy untouched the amount of space dedicated to this dimension.

Moving to the economic dimension, we can mostly observe dealignment phenomena among the parties in both terms of emphasis and position. In terms of emphasis, both the League and Forward Italy reduce the amount of space to dedicate to this topic, while Brothers of Italy rather prefers to dedicate more space to it. Moreover, we can observe that there is disagreement among these parties, for the first time, on how to position in the conflict of marketism vs. protectionism. On the one hand, both the League and Brothers of Italy clearly stand on the dichotomy 'Protectionism' recommending protectionist proposals to "enhance the quality of our *know-how* and our industrial excellence" (League, 2018) and the "protection of our strategic assets and our production capacity from foreign aggression" (Brothers of Italy, 2018). On the other hand, Forward Italy, in line with its laissez-faire tradition, stands in favor of the dichotomy 'marketism' as it still favors proposals in defense of the neo-liberal economic model.

Finally, in the cultural dimension, the parties still show phenomena of both alignment and dealignment. On the one hand, all three parties are strongly aligned over the dichotomy 'nativism'. Similar to the institutional dimension, both the League and Forward Italy drastically moved from a neutral position to a strong nativist position. Although they did not mention this topic in 2013, they strongly opposed multiculturalism in 2018 by making the naturalization process of foreigners born in Italy or the application process for asylum even more difficult. For instance, the League (2018) demanded "not only the 10-year residence but also an examination of knowledge of the Italian language, culture and traditions, for the purpose of evaluating overall integration". Similarly, Forward Italy (2018) proposed to abolish the asylum request describing it as an "Italian anomaly of the indiscriminate granting of self-styled humanitarian protection". Again, Brothers of Italy demonstrates its programmatic coherence from 2013 to 2018, always standing on the dichotomy 'nativism' focusing on policies to achieve cultural homogeneity in society for a "full integration of new citizens" (Brothers of Italy, 2013) or rejecting minority groups' rights such as the creation of a "register of Imams and the obligation of sermons in Italian" (Brothers of Italy, 2018). Still, the parties show dealignment in terms of emphasis. In 2018, the League and Brothers of Italy dedicated a significant part of their manifestos to this topic (respectively 7% and 9%), while Forward Italy is more reluctant reaching only 2%.

These results demonstrate the differences and similarities between the right-wing parties with regard to the new transnational cleavage. Although Brothers of Italy remained coherent from 2013 to 2018, one can observe that both the League and Forward Italy have a pivotal role in drastically changing the nature of the center-right coalition with regards to transnational cleavage especially within the institutional and the cultural dimensions. In fact, the League and Forward Italy have reshaped the Italian center-right coalition, ceasing to support the European integration process (as they traditionally used to do) and also started to explicitly address the cultural dimension aligning with the radical positions of the Brothers of Italy. This realignment process of the League and Forward Italy is the basis of placing the Italian center-right coalition in the pantheon of Euroskeptic movements in Europe. However, it should be noted that, within the economic dimension, Forward Italy does not completely align with the other two radical right parties as it remains an entrepreneurial party and, per its nature, it is bounded by its neo-liberal economic tradition.

Conclusion

Analyzing the Italian party system at both the country and party levels, we have shown that the multidimensional issues can offer a crucial understanding of the political debate around transnational cleavage. In fact, the threefold dimensions constituting this new ideological conflict offer an opportunity for a more detailed investigation of how it developed within Italian public opinion, between the two Italian coalitions challenging each other and among the Italian right-wing parties that founded the center-right coalition from 2013 to 2018. The analysis confirmed the idea that transnational cleavage is better understood if framed based on three core dimensions, showing that both individuals and parties do not usually have clear-cut strategies. However, they can employ elements from both Euroskepticism and Europeanism. Moreover, this innovative reconceptualization of transnational cleavage shows which dimension is more responsible for shaping new societal divisions within public opinion and which new political opportunities are available for competing political parties.

Our results suggest that the institutional dimension of transnational cleavage is the conflict that mostly contributes to the polarization process of transnational cleavage between pro-EU vs. anti-EU within the Italian party system. In fact, at the individual level, regardless of the positive attitudes of both the economic and cultural dimensions tending to increase in 2019, most Italians have lost confidence with regard to the European integration process from an institutional perspective. Italians do not see the European institutions as reliable any more to handle major crises, but they rather prefer to have 'back the control' of national sovereignty. At the party level, since 2008, the two coalitions have started to distinguish each other with regards to new transnational cleavage especially within its economic dimension (since 2008). However, the European issue became even more polarizing at the party level in the 2018 general elections thanks to the institutional dimension where the center-left and the center-right coalitions diverge against each other as, respectively, 'European federalist' and 'National Souverainisme'. Moreover, from these analyses, we could show that the right-wing coalition has been 'radicalized' from one election to another moving from a utilitarian Europeanism toward a pure Euroskepticism. The political actors that are mostly responsible for this change are the oldest parties constituting the center-right coalition: the League and Forward Italy. In fact, in 2013, both parties balanced the strong antagonization of the Brothers of Italy[117] against the EU especially within the institutional dimension when they used to stand for the dichotomy 'European federalism'. However, in the last general election (2018), both the League and Forward Italy shifted to strongly antagonize the *political* European integration process, embracing the dichotomy 'National Souverainisme'. We believe that the reason behind the realignment of the more moderate right-wing forces was to intercept the rising discontent of Italian public opinion toward the European institutions considered as distant from the Italian citizens' needs. Indeed, in line with previous research (Vasilopoulou, 2018), in times of crisis, the EU is often discredited by electors and right-wing parties (radical and mainstream) for Brussels' unpopular political decisions when handling global issues. More specifically, the Italian people blamed Brussels for the implementation of austerity policies during the

---

[117] We must also recall that Brothers of Italy can be considered as a 'new' political party since it was founded around the new transnational cleavage structure theorised by Hooghe and Marks (2018).

economic crisis and are still blaming the EU for abandoning the Italian state from the so-called "invasions" of migrants from Northern Africa (Conti et al., 2020).

The implications of this new political landscape are manifold. First, this new ideological conflict can be at the basis of new national alliances[118] that would have been unpredicted so far through the lens of more classical conflicts (e.g., the alliance between the League and the Five Stars Movement). Second, the 'radicalization' of the center-right coalition with regard to the European discourse can provoke new political ramifications that might aggravate the current political balances at the European level—just consider that the European center-right and center-left have always been allies in the European parliament. Third, if one of the founding countries of the EU, like Italy, undertakes a strategy of obstructing international cooperation/solidarity at the European level from within or, in its worst scenario, the Italian government might incite the withdrawal of Italy from European membership, there might be unpredictable and irreversible long-term impacts on the European integration process as a whole.

References

Anderson, J. J. (2021). A Series of Unfortunate Events: Crisis Response and the European Union After 2008. In Riddervold, M., Trondal, J., & Newsome, A. (Eds.). *The Palgrave handbook of EU crises*. Cham: Palgrave Macmillan.

Barbulescu R. and Beaudonnet L. (2014). Protecting Us, Protecting Europe? Public Concern about Immigration and Declining Support for European Integration in Italy, *Perspectives on European Politics and Society*, 15(2), 216-237.

Baumgartner, F. R., and Jones, B. D. (Eds.). (2002). *Policy dynamics*. Chicago: University of Chicago Press.

---

[118] For instance, the main outcome of the 2018 general elections produced the I Conte Cabinet, which was an alliance between the League and the Five Stars Movement that, for the very first time in the Italian history, created an openly populist and Euroskeptic government.

Bellucci P. (2014). The Political Consequences of Blame Attribution for the Economic Crisis in the 2013 Italian National Election. Journal of Elections, Public Opinion & Parties, 24(2), 243-263.

Brunazzo, M., and Mascitelli, B. (2020). At the origin of Italian Euroskepticism. *Australian and New Zealand Journal of European Studies*, 12(2).

Conti, N., Marangoni, F., and Verzichelli, L. (2020). Euroskepticism in Italy from the Onset of the Crisis: Tired of Europe?. *South European Society and Politics*, 1-26.

Crespy, A., and Verschueren, N. (2009). From Euroskepticism to resistance to European integration: An interdisciplinary perspective. *Perspectives on European politics and society*, 10(3), 377-393.

Daniels P. (1998). Italy in European Union, *Economic and Political Weekly*, 33(35).

Eichenberg, R. C., and Dalton, R. J. (2007). Post-Maastricht blues: The transformation of citizen support for European integration, 1973-2004. *Acta politica*, 42(2), 128-152.

Emanuele, V., Marino, B., and Angelucci, D. (2020). The congealing of a new cleavage? The evolution of the demarcation bloc in Europe (1979–2019). *Italian Political Science Review*, 50(3), 314-333.

Feld W. and Wildgen J. (1976). *Domestic Political Realities and European Unification*, Boulde. CO: Westview.

Gattinara, P. C. (2016). *The Politics of Migration in Italy: Perspectives on local debates and party competition*. Routledge.

Geddes, A., and Pettrachin, A. (2020). Italian migration policy and politics: Exacerbating paradoxes. *Contemporary Italian Politics*, 12(2), 227-242.

Handley D. (1981). Public opinion and European integration: the crisis of the 1970S. *European Journal of Political Research*, 9, 335-364.

Hooghe, L., and Marks, G. (2009). A postfunctionalist theory of European integration: From permissive consensus to constraining dissensus. *British journal of political science*, 39(1), 1-23.

Hooghe, L., and Marks, G. (2018). Cleavage theory meets Europe's crises: Lipset, Rokkan, and the transnational cleavage. *Journal of European public policy*, 25(1), 109-135.

Kertzer, D. I. (2015). Interview with Romano Prodi: Part Two: from the fall of the first Prodi government (1998), Prodi's term as President of the European Commission (1999–2004), the second Prodi government (2006–08) and Italy's 2013 presidential elections. *Journal of Modern Italian Studies*, 20(4), 508-526.

Kopecký, P., and Mudde, C. (2002). The two sides of Euroskepticism: Party positions on European integration in East Central Europe. *European Union Politics*, 3(3), 297-326.

Kriesi, H., and Grande, E. (2015). The Europeanization of the national political debate. *Democratic politics in a European Union under stress*, 67-86.

Laver, M. J., & Budge, I. (1992). Measuring policy distances and modelling coalition formation. In *Party policy and government coalitions* (pp. 15-40). London: Palgrave Macmillan.

Leruth, B., Startin, N. and Usherwood, S. M. D. (Eds) (2018). *The Routledge handbook of Euroskepticism*. Abingdon, Oxon: Routledge.

Leupold, A. (2015), A Structural Approach to Politicisation in the Euro Crisis. *West European Politics*, 39:1.

Lindberg, L. and Scheingold S. (1970), *Europe's Would-Be Polity*, Englewood Cliffs, NJ: Prentice Hall.

Lipset S. M. and Rokkan S. (1967). Cleavage structures, Party Systems and Voter Alignments: An Introduction. *Party Systems and Voter Alignments*. New York: The Free Press, 1-64.

Marks, G., Wilson, C. J., and Ray, L. (2002). National political parties and European integration. *American Journal of Political Science*, 585-594.

McLaren, L. (2002). Public Support for the European Union: Cost/Benefit Analysis or Perceived Cultural Threat?, *The Journal of Politics*, 64(2), 551-566.

Mudde, C. (2007). *Populist radical right parties in Europe*. Cambridge: Cambridge University Press.

Mudde, C. (2012). The comparative study of party-based Euroskepticism: the Sussex versus the North Carolina School. *East European Politics*, 28(2), 193-202.

Mueller, W. (2010). The Soviet Union and Early West European Integration, 1947-1957: From the Brussels Treaty to the ECSC and the EEC. *JEIH Journal of European Integration History*, 15(2), 67-86.

Rydgren, J. (2007). The sociology of the radical right. *Annu. Rev. Sociol.*, 33, 241-262.

Schimmelfennig, F., and Sedelmeier, U. (2002). Theorizing EU enlargement: research focus, hypotheses, and the state of research. *Journal of European public policy*, 9(4), 500-528.

Scipioni, M. (2018). Failing forward in EU migration policy? EU integration after the 2015 asylum and migration crisis. *Journal of European Public Policy*, 25(9), 1357-1375.

Serricchio, F. (2012). Italian citizens and Europe: Explaining the growth of Euroskepticism. *Bulletin of Italian Politics*, 4(1), 115-134.

Spiering, M. (2004). British Euroskepticism. In R. Harmsen and M. Spiering (Eds.) *Euroskepticism: Party Politics, National Identity and European Integration* (pp. 127-149). Amsterdam, New York: Rodopi.

Szczerbiak, A. and Taggart, P. A. (2008). *Opposing Europe? Volume 2, Comparative and Theoretical Perspectives: The Comparative Party Politics of Euroskepticism.* Oxford: Oxford University Press.

Taggart, P. (1998). A touchstone of dissent: Euroskepticism in contemporary Western European party systems. *European Journal of Political Research,* 33(3), 363-388.

Tsebelis, G., and Geoffrey G. (2000), Legislative Politics in the European Union. *European Union Politics,* 1:1, 9-36.

Varsori, A. (2010). *La cenerentola d'Europa. L'Italia e l'integrazione europea dal 1947 a oggi.* Soveria Mannelli: Rubbettino Editore.

Werner, A., Lacewell, O., and Volkens, A. (2011). Manifesto Coding Instructions (4th fully revised edition), URl: http://goo.gl/g512Q.

Chapter 7
One Year on from the 2022 Italian General Election

This final chapter explores the main factors that have characterized the current Italian political landscape. This is the research phenomenon that authors of party politics define as the mainstreaming of the radical right. To provide a detailed overview of what this phenomenon is and how this is linked to the future of Italian politics, this chapter is structured into two main sections. The first section will provide details of what is the mainstreaming of the radical right. The chapter then proceeds by exploring the first year of Meloni's coalition government as a case study to explain how the mechanism of radical right mainstreaming occurs through the analysis of the political campaign that culminated in the Brothers of Italy's (FdI) victory in the September 25, 2022 general election. The chapter then discusses how FdI managed to secure 26% of the overall vote share and take part in a broader right-wing coalition government that achieved 44% of the votes. The chapter then concludes by exploring the subsequent formation of the Meloni government and outlines the challenges that lay ahead for the Meloni government in the future.

The mainstreaming of the radical right: a global phenomenon that involves Italy

In contemporary political landscapes, we are currently witnessing the emergence of a new political elite whose foundational values and ideas were historically marginalized in the aftermath of World War II. This phenomenon, commonly referred to as the resurgence of far-right ideologies, is alternatively characterized as a cultural backlash (Norris and Inglehart, 2019) or the onset of a third wave of far-right movements (Mudde, 2019). Norris and Inglehart (2019) expound upon the predicament faced by the majority ethnic group in Western societies, predominantly comprising aging white male working-class individuals. They contend that these individuals increasingly perceive themselves as persecuted or marginalized within their own nations due to the progressive and cosmopolitan policies of the past three decades, aimed at safeguarding and integrating various minority groups — ethnic, religious, gender, and sexual, among others — under the banner of the rule of law.

Over the years, Western society has undergone a transformation characterized by a post-materialistic wave commencing in the mid-1970s. However, this wave has given way to a counter-narrative that seeks to revive erstwhile disregarded values and ideas, including nativism, authoritarianism, and antagonism toward liberal democratic principles, including the protection of minority groups (Palano, 2020). Simultaneously, the persistent economic recession and financial crises that have plagued Western societies in the last two decades have manifested themselves predominantly through electoral support for far-right political parties. This phenomenon, as described by Mudde (2019), is known as the mainstreaming of the radical right. We are currently traversing a historical epoch in which previously stigmatized ideas, such as those embraced by far-right movements, are no longer marginalized but have been internalized by society, marking the process of mainstreaming. The mainstreaming of the radical right can occur along two distinct trajectories. First, it can involve the normalization of parties that were once pariahs, shunned by society for their extreme right-wing ideologies. These parties have now gained acceptance and integration into civil society. The second form of mainstreaming is the radicalization of mainstream right-wing parties, a phenomenon often attributed to their strategy to capture the electorate of ascendant radical right parties. In this context, the ideas and values previously considered extreme have evolved into an acceptable part of the democratic discourse (Campati, 2022; Palano, 2024).

Considering the scholarly discourse outlined above, the following section will delve into the Italian case. Italy, exemplified by the government led by Giorgia Meloni, provides an intriguing political laboratory that embodies the normalization of far-right ideas.

The FdI in government: September 2022–September 2023

During the summer of 2022, FdI prepared for the September 25 election with an overall low-profile campaign, if one excludes a couple of very controversial tweets on August 22 (later partially retracted) that produced strong controversy. The first concerned the role of sport in confronting an unspecified concept of deviance[119], and the second, a blacked-out film of a man, a 27-year-old asylum seeker originally from Guinea, raping a 55-year-old Ukrainian woman on the street in Piacenza[120]. Regarding the institutions of the EU, historical allies (NATO first and foremost) and financial markets, FdI has avoided any pretext that might lend itself to controversy.

Focusing on a few key elements of the political platform for the general election (FdI, 2022). The manifesto's first point, "support for birth and family", calls for the launch of "communication and information campaigns of a medical nature on the subject of fertility", among other things. Family is the focus of the manifesto's first point throughout, beginning with the birth rate (FdI, 2022: 5–6). In the following points (2, 3, 4, and 5), which are collectively titled "Made in Italy and Italian Pride", it is discussed how to allocate PNRR funds differently considering "new circumstances", "a new relationship between the tax authorities and taxpayers", and "support for the Italian entrepreneurial system". Point 9 mentions the abolition of the *reddito di cittadinanza* state-guaranteed minimum income and an extraordinary public-private housing plan, while point 12 mentions that 'the laws on civil unions will be maintained' while 'the ban on same-sex adoptions and the fight against surrogate motherhood, in the supreme interest of the child, is reiterated'. Point 13 (p. 22) is very interesting, referring to the "creation of a new Italian consciousness by promoting, particularly in schools, the

---

[119] Devianze giovanili, polemica Meloni-Letta. Fratelli d'Italia inserisce obesità e anoressia, poi ritratta. Repubblica. From https://www.repubblica.it/politica/20 22/08/22/news/devianze_meloni_letta_fdi_tweet_polemiche-362596517/
[120] Meloni posta sui social il video dello stupro di Piacenza, è polemica. Letta: "Indecente". Sky tg24. From https://tg24.sky.it/politica/2022/08/22/giorgia-meloni-stupro-piacenza-video

history of Italy's greats and historical reenactments" and "countering cancel culture and the iconoclasm that threaten the symbols of our identity". Points 14, 15 and 16 deal respectively with the value of tourism and the agri-food sector, and the protection of the environment and nature. Points 17, 18 and 19 deal with investments in affordable clean energy, and in infrastructure and transport. Point 21, on the other hand, speaks of "stopping illegal immigration" and of "an increasingly insecure Italy", with the consequent need for "the defence of national and European borders, as envisaged by the Schengen Treaty and the EU, with border control and a blockade of landings to stop, in agreement with the North African authorities, the trafficking of human beings; the creation of hotspots in non-European territories, managed by the EU, to assess asylum requests, and the fair distribution only of those with rights in the 27 member countries (naval blockade)". The last two points are also of particular interest, referring to the reform (the dynamics are not well specified) in a presidential sense of the state (point 24) to achieve greater stability of government and greater economic growth, and a new leading role for Italy in Europe and the world (point 25), with full respect for international alliances, "including by adapting the appropriations for Defence to the parameters agreed in the Atlantic Alliance" (Bruno, 2022b: 178-179).

At the Italian general election held on September 25, 2022, FdI was the undisputed winner (Chiaramonte and De Sio, 2024). As Bruno has pointed out (2022b, 18-19), the election was characterized by a high level of abstention (the lowest turnout ever recorded at under 64% overall) and saw the victory of the right-wing coalition, with 43.79% and 44.02% of the vote share overall (obtained respectively in the Chamber of the Deputies and the Senate of the Republic). The party led by Giorgia Meloni obtained in both Houses an excellent performance with around 26%, while Matteo Salvini's Lega emerged greatly weakened at around 8.8%, followed closely by Silvio Berlusconi's FI, slightly above 8%. On the other hand, the center-left coalition, led by the PD of Enrico Letta, reached about 26% in the two Houses of Parliament, the Movimento Cinque Stelle, led by Giuseppe Conte 15.5% and Azione-Italia Viva about 7.7%.

Table 7.1   Electoral performances for Italian coalitions at 2022 (and comparison with 2018)

	% 2022 general election*	% 2018 general election*	% difference 2018-2022
Right-wing coalition	43.79	37	+6.79
Center-left coalition	26.13	22.86	+3.27
Terzo Polo	7.79	-	-
M5S	15.43	32.68	-17.43

Notes: The percentage of the Italian 2018 and 2022 general elections refers to the Chamber of Deputies.

Overall, the victory of the right-wing coalition was less overwhelming than expected, as in the past, similar Berlusconi-led coalitions have reached as high as 48%, thereby showing a certain continuity (Albertazzi et al. 2021). It is undeniable that there has been an intra-coalition balance shift, continuing a process that had already begun several years ago (Albertazzi and Zulianello, 2022; Castelli Gattinara and Froio, 2021). Thus, while it is undeniable that within the right-wing coalition, there has been a turnover from Berlusconi to Salvini and from Salvini to Meloni, with some radicalization, it is also unlikely, as proposed by many media outlets, especially international media, that most Italians have become extreme right-wing sympathizers within a few years. As well argued by Vassallo and Vignati (2023) through analysis of vote flows, FdI has absorbed the bulk of the votes lost by Lega in a zero-sum game (Albertazzi and Zulianello 2022; Bruno 2022b).

Table 7.2   Electoral performances for main Italian parties between 2014 and 2022 (general elections and EP elections)

	% 2014 EP election	% 2018 general election*	% 2019 EP election	% 2022 general election*
FdI	3.67	4.35	6.44	26
Lega	6.15	17.35	34.26	8.77
Forza Italia	16.81	14	8.78	8.11
PD	40.81	18.76	22.74	19.07
M5S	21.6	32.68	17.06	15.43

Notes: The percentage of the Italian 2018 and 2022 general elections refers to the Chamber of Deputies.

On 22 October 2022, the new Meloni government was sworn in and took office, with the Draghi government remaining in charge of current affairs after resigning on July 21. Overall, the Meloni government is comprised of ten members of the FdI, five members of Lega, five members of FI and five independents (a total, including the PM, of seven women out of 25 ministers)[121].

Table 7.3 List of the ministries comprising the Meloni government

Government Role	Politician
Presidente del Consiglio dei Ministri (PM)	Giorgia Meloni (1977-), FdI
Vice Presidenti del Consiglio dei Ministri (Deputy PMs)	
Vice President of the Council of Ministers	Matteo Salvini (1973-), Lega
Vice President of the Council of Ministers	Antonio Tajani (1953-), Forza Italia
Ministri con Portafoglio	
Ministro degli affari esteri e della cooperazione internazionale	Antonio Tajani (1953-), Forza Italia
Ministro dell'interno	Matteo Piantedosi (1963-), Independent/Lega
Ministro della giustizia	Carlo Nordio (1947-), FdI
Ministro della difesa	Guido Crosetto (1963-), FdI
Ministro dell'economia e delle finanze	Giancarlo Giorgetti (1966-), Lega
Ministro delle imprese e del made in Italy	Adolfo Urso (1957-), FdI
Ministro dell'agricoltura, della sovranità alimentare e delle foreste	Francesco Lollobrigida (1972-), FdI
Ministro dell'ambiente e della sicurezza energetica	Gilberto Pichetto Fratin (1954-), Forza Italia
Ministro delle infrastrutture e dei trasporti	Matteo Salvini (1973-), Lega
Ministro del lavoro e delle politiche sociali	Marina Elvira Calderone (1965-), Independent
Ministro dell'istruzione e merito	Giuseppe Valditara (1961-), Lega

---

[121] https://www.governo.it/it/articolo/i-ministri-del-governo-meloni/20676

Ministro dell'università e ricerca	Anna Maria Bernini (1965-), Forza Italia
Ministro della cultura	Gennaro Sangiuliano (1962-), Independent/FdI
Ministro della salute	Orazio Schillaci (1966-), Independent
Ministro del turismo	Daniela Santanchè (1961-), FdI
Ministri senza Portafoglio	
Ministro per i rapporti con il Parlamento	Luca Ciriani (1967-), FdI
Ministro per la pubblica amministrazione	Paolo Zangrillo (1961-), Forza Italia
Ministro affari regionale ed autonomie	Roberto Calderoli (1956-), Lega
Ministro per la protezione civile e le politiche del mare	Nello Musumeci (1955-), FdI
Ministro per gli affari europei, le politiche di coesione e il PNRR	Raffaele Fitto (1969-), FdI
Ministro per lo sport e i giovani	Andrea Abodi (1960-), Independent
Ministro per la famiglia, la natalità e le pari opportunità	Eugenia Maria Roccella (1953-), FdI
Ministro per la disabilità	Alessandra Locatelli (1976-), Lega
Ministro per le riforme istituzionali	Maria Elisabetta Alberti Casellati (1946-), Forza Italia

On October 13 2022, Ignazio La Russa (FdI) was elected as the new president of the Italian Senate, while the day after, Lorenzo Fontana (Lega) was elected as the new president of the Italian Chamber of the Deputies, provoking controversy over the radical positions held by the two presidents in the past[122]. For instance, Ignazio La Russa publicly declared having a bust of Mussolini at home and considered himself anti-Fascist. Lorenzo Fontana, former minister for the

---

[122] Ignazio La Russa e Lorenzo Fontana, presidenti che dividono. Repubblica. From: https://www.repubblica.it/commenti/2022/10/15/news/fontana_camera_la_russa_senato_governo_meloni-370077580/. As written by Claudio Tito on Italy's newspaper Repubblica on La Russa and Fontana: 'One is perceived as the upholder of a past tradition. The other is publicly a Putinian, a detractor of the EU and an enemy of civil rights that are considered inalienable in Europe."

family and disabilities, had sponsored the organization of the World Family Congress in 2019 in Verona by the ultraconservative group ProVita & Famiglia. Consequently, as extreme positions become increasingly acceptable, society is less likely to condemn or oppose them. This normalization can also extend to hatred and discrimination, as people may perceive them as acceptable, resulting in increased discrimination and violence against minority groups.

Among the first acts of the Meloni government were telephone calls with Ukrainian President Zelensky (October 28). Subsequently, on October 31 2022, the executive approved a single decree with urgent regulations on justice (with a rule regarding hostile life imprisonment), health (the measure of suspension from practice in case of non-compliance with the obligation to vaccinate against COVID-19 eliminated, regarding the category of health professionals) and especially on public order, with the so-called 'rave decree', by which the rules on the invasion of land or buildings, public or private, are amended, with the provision of imprisonment from three to six years and a fine from 1000 to 10,000 euros, if the act is committed by more than 50 persons for the purpose of organizing a gathering from which a danger to public order or public safety or public health may result and provides for the confiscation of the things used to commit the offense[123]. Among the government's measures is also replacing the citizenship income, a workhorse of M5S passed in 2018, with a new tool called 'Mia' (Active Inclusion Measure), with a reduction of the subsidy with stricter rules on job offers and the possibility of rejecting them.

The Meloni government's decree on immigrants provided harsher penalties for so-called smugglers (i.e., those who are identified as drivers of the boat) and introduced the new crime of 'death or injury as a result of illegal immigration crimes', with penalties of ten to 20 years for serious or very serious injury to one or more persons; 15 to 24 years for the death of one person; and 20 to 30 years for the death of several persons. It thus speeds up the execution of

---

[123] Decreto rave: ok definitivo dalla Camera con la ghigliottina. Ansa. From: https://www.ansa.it/sito/notizie/politica/2022/12/30/decreto-rave-ok-definitivo-dalla-camera_305d1947-3c2a-4c3d-9d61-b94095ec3980.html

deportation decrees. It amends special protection, the humanitarian residence permit (introduced in 2020 by Minister Luciana Lamorgese's decree, which in turn amended Salvini's 2018 security decree). This is a residence permit for humanitarian reasons in which the person's degree of integration is assessed. Finally, rules are introduced to manage reception centers and hotspots according to emergency principles. The government has planned to 'derogate from the public contracts code, allowing for greater speed in the conduct of procedures' when it comes to opening or expanding detention centers for repatriation[124].

Concerning Italy's foreign policy under the Meloni executive, there is strong continuity with the Draghi executive, judging by the positioning on Ukraine. Therefore, this can be interpreted as a sign of continuity, politically speaking. In fact, during both the general election campaign and after the election victory, Meloni reiterated that Italy under her government would in no way represent the weak link of Europeanism and Atlanticism in the West. We have seen that the party most opposed to sending arms to Ukraine is currently the Five Star Movement, in substantial continuity with (some of) the motivations that contributed to the fall of the Draghi government.

Lega and FI, on the other hand, continue to move somewhat inconsistently and unevenly, with statements often against sending arms and other support to Ukraine that are then downplayed and/or denied by the official organs of the two parties. This dossier may likely contribute to future crises within the current governing majority. In fact, FdI has always stated (even at the level of its electoral program) that it will continue supporting Ukraine, in substantial continuity with what it has said since the beginning of the conflict at the end of February 2022. The PD led by Elly Schlein is currently in a 'waiting' phase. Although Letta's line of strong support for Ukraine was in line substantially with the actions of Mario Draghi, and his government has prevailed so far, the PD is, internally, a very divided party. Finally, the Third Pole consisting of the

---

[124] https://www.governo.it/it/articolo/conferenza-stampa-del-consiglio-dei-ministri-n-24-lintroduzione-del-presidente-meloni/22020

parties of Renzi and Calenda, remains a big supporter of the 'Draghi agenda' and support for Ukraine, including on the level of armaments to be shipped to Kyiv. To conclude, as far as the 'Ukraine dossier' is concerned, the transition between the technocratic government of national unity led by Mario Draghi and the right-wing political government led by Giorgia Meloni seems, for the time being, to have taken place under the sign of continuity. However, only the months to come will confirm whether this holds true or not and whether the current alignment will allow the right-wing coalition to persist (Bruno and Fazio, 2023).

In August 2023, the Meloni government unexpectedly announced a one-time tax on the extra profits of Italian banks, provoking turmoil on Italy's benchmark stock market index, heavily composed of banks.[125] The decision was allegedly made in response to the season of high-interest rate hikes decided by the ECB, which led to an increase in variable-rate mortgages. The aim of the tax was allegedly for 'social justice', with the proceeds then going to help first home mortgages and reduce taxes. The rate charged would have been forty percent, based on several factors, including the interest margin for previous years (*Ansa* August 9, 2023)[126]. The majority (e.g., Matteo Salvini, who endorsed the measure in the name of 'fairness') and the opposition in the Italian Parliament have been surprisingly in agreement in appreciating the measure to protect families and support those struggling to pay their mortgages.

While almost all majority and opposition parties welcomed the tax, except for FI and Italia Viva and Azione (*Repubblica*, August 15, 2023)[127], it immediately raised perplexity by analysts, both regarding the modality and the instrument in itself. The tax was announced unexpectedly and suddenly in the middle of the summer; there had been no debate, neither at the level of parliament nor

---

[125] In the first month of the current legislature, there have been talks of the possibility for the Italian Ministry of Economy and Finance (MEF) to launch a bond conceived *only* for Italian citizens. However, for the time being, the possibility has not been concretized yet.

[126] https://www.ansa.it/sito/notizie/economia/2023/08/08/banche-come-funziona-la-tassa-sugli-extraprofitti_fc620ed7-33b6-4e2c-9e96-a7ffef7212e8.html

[127] https://www.repubblica.it/politica/2023/08/15/news/tajani_forza_italia_meloni_colloquio-411131375/.

public opinion, on the issue. As for the measure itself, as Tajani himself highlighted among others, the tax, as conceived originally, would have hit both large and small Italian banks at the same rate, also having dangerous effects at the level of Italian public debt (as already mentioned, currently at 140% of Italy's GDP), which Italian banks regularly buy.

Unsurprisingly, international financial markets did not welcome the news[128]. In particular, the Italian Stock Exchange, where the banking sector is the most important component, including banks such as Unicredit, Intesa and Fineco, posted significant declines, with the FTSE MIB (*Milano Indice di Borsa*), the benchmark stock market index for the *Borsa Italiana* (the Italian national stock exchange) opening in negative territory and suffering losses of around 10 billion euros. The original version of the tax assumed a one-time rate of forty percent applied when the interest margin, i.e., the difference between interest income and interest expense, recorded in 2022 exceeds the value of the 2021 fiscal year by at least three percent. Moreover, if it does so by at least six percent in 2023 compared to 2022 ('linearity' is, in this sense, effectively a total lack of equalization), the model apparently chosen by the Giorgia Meloni-led executive would cut without making any distinctions. Second, the tax missed, in its original version, any kind of distinction in terms of size, seemingly neglecting the role of financial institutions deemed as 'too big to fail' (see Chesney 2018 and Dembinski 2009).

Considering how the Meloni government has governed in the last year, the rationale behind the sudden decision to tax the extra profits of Italian banks without any prior notice, or having consulted the parties involved nor having informed the ECB and other European authorities seems even less understandable. Shortly afterwards, the tax was immediately and sharply scaled back, with the Italian Ministry of Economy and Finance (MEF), led by Giancarlo Giorgetti (Lega), stating that the amount owed by

---

[128] And yet, in reality, the model of the tax closely traces the one pioneered by the Draghi government on energy companies to recover resources for businesses and households against high energy prices.

individual institutions will not be allowed to exceed 0.1 percent of their capital assets, that is, of all the assets that banks hold. The move that followed twenty-four hours after the first announcement brought the maximum revenue from the tax down to less than four billion euros, but it is likely to be less, much less than the eight to ten billion that was originally planned[129]. The sum gained would be ideally used by the Italian government to finance the first-home mortgage fund, intended for citizens aged under 36 planning to buy homes, and to finance a non-better-specified tax cut[130] (*Sky Tg24*, August 9, 2023). Following two months of intense debate, in Italy, but also at the EU level, concerning the tax on the bank's extra profits, and despite being acclaimed by almost all of Italy's political parties, including the opposition, the Meloni government opted to further downsize the tax in late September 2023. Therefore, Italian banks will either pay the tax *or* set aside a reserve in their overall assets. The government's latest amendment stipulates that Italian credit institutions can opt to divert the contribution to capital strengthening, *de facto* pleasing Italian banks and at the same time the ECB whilst saving the face of the government (ANSA September 23, 2023)[131].

Conclusion

The first year of the Meloni government, arguably the most right-wing executive in the history of the Italian Republic, has been marked by important continuity, in contrast to the Draghi executive and other past Italian executives. However, elements of great symbolic radicalness, cultural wars over immigration, ongoing civil

---

[129] For the country's two largest banks, the accounts would get smaller, with Intesa Sanpaolo expected to save over 1.5 billion euros compared to initial estimates, and Unicredit around 400 million.

[130] https://tg24.sky.it/economia/2023/08/09/tassa-extraprofitti-banche-rischi-conseguenze#:~:text=Il%20Ministero%20dell'Economia%20ridimensiona,beni%20che%20le%20banche%20possiedono.

[131] In precedence, pressing talks had been on guaranteeing that Italian banks will be able to claim credits over the next five to ten years, covering almost all of what they will have to disburse https://www.ansa.it/sito/notizie/economia/2023/09/23/banche-bozza-invece-di-tassa-si-puo-rafforzare-il-capitale_dd700f8d-8b57-43a6-b6fd-d0af6876a022.html.

rights issues and the rights of ethnic minorities remain key issues. Furthermore, it can be argued that the level of policies (such as the scaling back of citizenship income) and that of public narratives have remained both distinct and distant. Meloni's government has acted with great care not to seek confrontation with historical allies alongside regional and international institutions so far. Even at the economic and financial level, the executive and its ministers are aware of the precarious situation of Italy's public finances. Rather, it is a strategic action of gradual change from within the system that has been the hallmark of the government's work.

The only exception can be considered in August 2023, the 40% flat tax on Italian banks' extra profits, aiming for 'social justice', with the proceeds going to help first-time buyers and reducing the burden of other taxes[132]. Despite the support of almost all of Italy's political parties, including those in opposition, the tax on the extra profits of the banks will likely still be modified in the sense of diluting it, perhaps guaranteeing that Italian banks will be able to claim credits over the next five to ten years, covering almost all of what they will have to disburse, making it a well-disguised device. In addition, it is possible to ask whether this was not the government's original objective or whether it was an improvisation that was followed by equally sudden backtracking overall.[133]

The mainstreaming and normalization of radical-right ideas are multifaceted processes influenced by several factors. These processes carry significant implications for various aspects of society,

---

[132] While the majority (e.g., Matteo Salvini, who endorsed the measure in the name of 'fairness') and the opposition in the Italian Parliament are, surprisingly in agreement in appreciating the measure to protect families and support those struggling to pay their mortgages, not surprisingly financial markets did not welcome the news.

[133] Now, as far as we are concerned, we think it is more likely the latter option, particularly from the influence of some members of the government and the right-wing coalition supporting it. What makes us think in this direction is, once again, the ways in which the government led by Giorgia Meloni has acted so far, with great care not to seek confrontation with historical allies and regional and international institutions. Even at the economic and financial level, the executive and its ministers are aware of the precarious, to put it mildly, situation of Italy's public finance. Rather, it is a strategic action of gradual change, from within the system, that has been the hallmark of the government's work.

including political tolerance, freedom of speech, and the rise of far-right movements (Eremina and Seredenko, 2015; Ali, 2021). In this context, scholars on ultra-right terrorism in Western countries observe that this growth can be attributed to a multifaceted interplay of socioeconomic and spiritual crises, alongside a strategic shift employing 'anti-jihadism' narrative to legitimize their radical beliefs (Lowe, 2022; Kaunert et al., 2022). Rydgren (2005) has also delved into the rise in popularity of radical right ideologies. Rydgren (2005) points to factors such as the migration crisis, the spread of Islamophobia, and the impact of market-economic trends.

These elements have contributed to the expansion of radical-right ideas and movements, making the mainstreaming of such ideologies a global phenomenon. Furthermore, the normalization of narratives is rooted in the core features of radical-right ideologies, including nativism, authoritarianism, and hostility toward liberal democracy carries profound implications for democracies. The mainstreaming of radical-right ideas has far-reaching consequences, particularly on the fundamental principles that underpin liberal democratic societies. First and foremost, radical-right political parties often adopt a hostile stance toward minority groups and civil liberties, such as freedom of the press, expression, and association. When these parties ascend to government positions, they may enact policies that curtail or even eliminate these fundamental freedoms.

Orazani et al. (2020), for instance, conducted research revealing that the perceived normalization of radical ideologies, both on the right and left, correlates with a decrease in support for freedom of speech and an increase in political intolerance. Furthermore, radical-right ideologies tend to be inherently authoritarian and antidemocratic. This tendency often leads to attempts to limit democratic participation and political competition through various means (Palano, 2020). Such attempts may manifest as restrictions on political and civil rights, the use of violence or intimidation, or the enactment of laws that undermine political pluralism. Evident examples, such as the governance of radical right parties such as Fidesz in Hungary and the Law and Justice Party in Poland, demonstrate that once in power, these parties may maintain the rule of law and competitive elections. However, they may also prioritize the economic or political interests of the relative majority while repressing the rights of certain minority groups, be they political, cultural, or ethnic (Wintrobe, 2018: 218). In Hungary and Poland, excessive control by the relative majority over the relative minority across political, cultural, and ethnic dimensions has become evident. As a result, the mainstreaming of far-right ideologies can normalize hate and discrimination, potentially embedding them within the political and social fabric of a society. This normalization can lead to the emergence of a divided and polarized society where minority rights are disregarded, and the prevalence of violence becomes more pronounced.

The global mainstreaming of radical right ideas has far-reaching consequences for liberal democratic societies. These political ideologies, marked by hostility toward minorities and civil liberties, tend to lead to policies that curtail fundamental freedoms and limiting democratic participation. Hungary and Poland serve as examples where radical right parties prioritize the majority alongside suppressing minority rights. Considering the electoral success and normalization of radical-right parties such as the League and FdI, this normalization increases tolerance for hate and discrimination, further dividing Italian society along divided political lines between cosmopolitan values and radical-right values.

References

Albertazzi, D., and Zulianello, M. (2022). Italy's election is a case study in a new phase for the radical right. *The Conversation*. Available at: https://theconversation.com/italys-election-is-a-case-study-in-a-new-phase-for-the-radical-right-92198

Albertazzi, D., Bonansinga, A. and Zulianello, M. (2021). The right-wing alliance at the time of the Covid-19 pandemic: all change?. *Contemporary Italian Politics 13:2*, 181-195.

Ali, M. S. S. (2021). Far-right extremism in Europe. *Journal of European Studies (JES)*, 37(1), 119-139.

Bruno, V. A. (2022b). 'Center right? What center right?' Italy's right-wing coalition: Forza Italia's political 'heritage' and the mainstreaming of the far-right. In V. A. Bruno (Ed.), *Populism and Far-Right. Trends in Europe* (pp. 163-195). Milan: EDUCatt

Campati, Antonio (2022). *La distanza democratica. Corpi intermedi e rappresentanza politica.* Milano: Vita & Pensiero.

Castelli Gattinara, P., and Froio, C. (2021). Italy: the Mainstream Right and its Allies, 1994-2018. In T. Bale and C. Rovira Kaltwasser (Eds.)., *Riding the Populist Wave. Europe's Mainstream Right in Crisis.* Cambridge: Cambridge University Press.

Chesney, M. (2018). *A permanent crisis: The financial oligarchy's seizing of power and the failure of democracy.* Cham: Springer.

Chiaramonte, A. and De Sio, L. (Eds.) (2024). *Un polo solo. Le elezioni politiche del 2022.* Bologna: Il Mulino.

Dembinski, P. H. (2009). *Finance: Servant or Deceiver?.* Cham: Springer.

Eremina, N., and Seredenko, S. (2015). *Right Radicalism in Party and Political Systems in Present-day European States.* Cambridge: Cambridge Scholars Publishing.

Kaunert, C., de Deus Pereira, J., and Edwards, M. (2022). Thick Europe, ontological security and parochial Europe: the re-emergence of far-right extremism and terrorism after the refugee crisis of 2015. *European politics and society*, 23(1), 42-61.

Lowe, D. (2022). Far-right extremism: is it legitimate freedom of expression, hate crime, or terrorism?. *Terrorism and political violence*, 34(7), 1433-1453.

Mudde, C. (2019). *The far-right today.* Hoboken: John Wiley & Sons.

Norris, P., ands Inglehart, R. (2019). *Cultural backlash: Trump, Brexit, and authoritarian populism.* Cambridge: Cambridge University Press.

Orazani, S. N., Wohl, M. J., and Leidner, B. (2020). Perceived normalization of radical ideologies and its effect on political tolerance and support for freedom of speech. *Group Processes & Intergroup Relations*, 23(8), 1150-1170.

Palano, D. (2020). *Bubble Democracy. La fine del pubblico e la nuova polarizzazione.* Brescia: Scholé Morcelliana.

Palano, D. (2024). (Ed.) *Genealogie del populismo. Per la storia di un concetto paranoico.* Milano: Mimesis.

Rydgren, J. (2005). Is extreme right-wing populism contagious? Explaining the emergence of a new party family. *European journal of political research*, 44(3), 413-437.

Vassallo, S., and Vignati, R. (2023). *Fratelli di Giorgia. Il partito della destra nazional-conservatrice* (pp. 1-291). Bologna: Il Mulino.

Wintrobe R. (2018). An economic theory of a hybrid (competitive authoritarian or illiberal) regime. *Public Choice*, 177(3–4), 217–233.

List of Abbreviations

AN	Alleanza Nazionale
Btp	Buono del tesoro poliennale
Bund	Bundesanleihe
CHES	Chapel Hill Expert Survey
CPM	Comparative Manifesto Project
DC	Democrazia Cristiana
EB	Eurobarometer
EC	European Commission
ECB	European Central Bank
ECR	European Conservatives and Reformists
ECSC	European Coal and Steel Community
EEC	European Economic Community
EFD	Europe Freedom and Democracy
EP	European Parliament
EPP	European People Party
FdI	Fratelli d'Italia
FI	Forza Italia
FLI	Futuro e Libertà per l'Italia
FTSE MIB	Financial Times Stock Exchange Milano Indice di Borsa
ID	Identity and Democracy
IMF	International Monetary Fund
M5S	Movimento Cinque Stelle, also 5SM
MEF	Ministry of Economy and Finance
MEP	Member of European Parliament
MSI	Movimento Sociale Italiano
NATO	North Atlantic Treaty Organization
NGEU	Next Generation European Union
PCI	Partito Comunista Italiano
PD	Partito Democratico
PDL	Popolo delle Libertà
PM	Prime Minister/Primo Ministro
PNRR	Piano Nazionale di Ripresa e Resilienza
USA	United States of America

ibidem.eu